Sports Illustrated

CROSS-COUNTRY SKIING

THE SPORTS ILLUSTRATED LIBRARY

BOOKS ON TEAM SPORTS

*Baseball
*Basketball

Football: Defense
Football: Offense
Football: Quarterback

Ice Hockey
Pitching
*Soccer
Volleyball

BOOKS ON INDIVIDUAL SPORTS

*Bowling
*Cross-Country Skiing
Fly Fishing
*Golf
Handball
Horseback Riding
Judo
*Racquetball
*Running for Women

Skiing
Squash
Table Tennis
*Tennis
Track: Running Events
Track: Field Events
*Tumbling
Wrestling

*Women's Gymnastics
   I: The Floor Exercise
   Event
*Women's Gymnastics
   II: The Vaulting,
   Balance Beam and
   Uneven Parallel Bars
   Events

BOOKS ON WATER SPORTS

*Canoeing
Powerboating
*Scuba Diving

Skin Diving and Snorkeling
Small Boat Sailing
Swimming and Diving

SPECIAL BOOKS

*Backpacking
Dog Training

Safe Driving
Training with Weights

*Expanded Format

Sports Illustrated
CROSS-COUNTRY SKIING

by CASEY SHEAHAN
photographs by
Bill Jaspersohn and
Casey Sheahan

HARPER & ROW, PUBLISHERS, New York
Cambridge, Philadelphia, San Francisco, London
Mexico City, São Paulo, Sydney

Ted Wood: p. 8, 82 (right), 86, 116 (right), 118, 120, 155 (top), 168 (upper right); Tom Kelly: pp. 16 (top), 17 (upper right), 24 (top), 66 (left); David Madison: p. 18 (top); courtesy of the California State Library, Sacramento, pp. 21, 22; courtesy of the United States Skiing Association: p. 23; Jarl Omholt-Jensen: p. 24 (bottom); Jan Reynolds: p. 25 (top); Pam Penfold: p. 25 (bottom); Christopher Knight: pp. 3, 12; Richard Murphy: pp. 17 (left), 18 (bottom), 109, 154, 155 (bottom), 168 (upper left). For *Sports Illustrated*: Steve Hansen: p. 16 (bottom), 76, 110; Joern Gerdts: p. 24 (middle); George Tiedemann: p. 60; Graham Finlayson, p. 85 (bottom); Heinz Kluetmeier: pp. 146, 159, 163, 170; Tony Duffy: p. 183. All other photos by Casey Sheahan and Bill Jaspersohn.

FIRST EDITION

Designer: C. Linda Dingler

Library of Congress Cataloging in Publication Data

Sheahan, Casey
    Sports illustrated cross-country skiing.

    (The Sports illustrated library)
    1. Cross-country skiing. I. Sports illustrated
(Time, inc.) II. Title. III. Title: Cross-country
skiing. IV. Series.
GV855.3.S53 1983   796.93   83-47543
ISBN 0-06-015070-X   84 85 86 87 88   10 9 8 7 6 5 4 3 2 1
ISBN 0-06-091042-9 (pbk.)   84 85 86 87 88   10 9 8 7 6 5 4 3 2 1

Contents

Preface

A few years after I took up cross-country skiing, some friends and I shouldered racing skis in our packs and hiked 25 miles through mud, rain, and snow until we reached the 8,000-foot Kaibab Plateau: the North Rim of the Grand Canyon. The North Rim is terribly difficult to reach in midwinter because the 40-mile summer road from northern Arizona is closed, although every month or so a Park Service helicopter from the South Rim bridges the mile-deep Colorado River gorge to shatter the stillness and carry provisions to the rangers stationed there. The flight takes two minutes.

Neither the helicopter ride nor the tedious 40-mile summer road were options for my friends and me. Besides, we wanted to walk through the inner canyon and witness 4,000,000 years of geological history firsthand. But little did we realize that it would take two days from the time we left civilization to negotiate the maze of frozen waterfalls and landslides blocking our path and traverse the slippery ledges that serve as trails before perching—just as the clouds lifted—on top of one of the most beautiful vistas in the world. With skis on our feet we raced each other down the Kaibab Plateau's hiking trails by the light of the moon,

9

The author at the Grand Canyon, toting his cross-country gear to the next snowy trail.

watched snow fall in thousand-foot curtains against red canyon walls, and decided wholeheartedly that this was what cross-country skiing was all about.

This book follows a similar path through the occasionally confusing, multifaceted world of cross-country skiing. In this journey of sorts we'll pick cross-country skiing apart from top to bottom, explore its colorful history, and clear up any questions you may have about selecting gear, waxing, basic technique, and training for the ski season.

Mark Twain missed the mark, as it were, in his diatribes against book-writing. It's not so bad as long as you've got plenty of help. This book would not have been possible without the following people's assistance and advice. For help with the photography, here's to Ted Wood, David Madison, Tom Kelly, Richard Murphy, Heinz Kluetmeier, and Dan Glick. For their patience in modeling the skiing and training sequences, I owe a debt of gratitude to the captain of Team Granola, Tom Windle, and to Jon Wiesel of National Nordic Consultants, Cindy Duncan, Sean O'Malley, Peter Karns, Wayne Hanson, Susan Liebensperger, Jay Moody, Paul Petersen, Wally Naylor, Kim Svendsen, Elizabeth Menendez, Brett Layser, Caren Jimenez, Debra Givner, Frances Wiesel, Pam Jaspersohn, and Christine Sherry. For their inspiration and encouragement, special thanks to Bob Woodward, John Fry, John Dostal, and Bill Jaspersohn (who has been instrumental in guiding this book to a shelf in the Sports Illustrated Library).

Finally, this book is dedicated to Sylvia Ricci for her help and understanding throughout this project.

Sports Illustrated
CROSS-COUNTRY SKIING

1

The Evolution of Today's Cross-Country Skier

Cross-country skiing is North America's fastest growing winter sport. Between 1970 and today, the number of participants has exploded from fifty thousand to more than six million. In the same period, the number of cross-country touring centers with ski rentals, warming facilities, and machine-packed trails has skyrocketed from less than twenty to more than five hundred. Not bad for an activity that's been around since the dawn of recorded history when ancient Scandinavians first used skis on hunting expeditions. Question is: For such an old sport, why the sudden surge of interest?

A good deal of the modern enthusiasm for cross-country skiing springs from the desire to get outdoors in winter and explore nature. This explains why so many ski tourers are summer hikers and backpackers—and vice versa. Winter is undoubtedly the best time to experience the serenity of our shrinking wilderness during its least populated season.

The fitness boom is also responsible. Sports-medicine authorities rate cross-country skiing better than any other sport known to man at providing cardiovascular benefit. Here's an activity that calls on almost every muscle in the body to per-

13

Fun with family and friends: from New England to California, millions have discovered the healthy benefits of cross-country skiing.

form a simple but graceful movement that's as natural as running but not nearly so harmful to joints and tendons.

Talk about accessibility! You can ski anywhere that there is six inches of snow on the ground—your backyard, a nearby state forest, or an organized ski touring center with marked, groomed trails (on which the snow is packed by machines into narrow tracks so your skis glide more easily than they do on ungroomed trails with deep snow and obstacles). Today's skier is just as likely to ski in tracks as not, and ironically, skiing today can be as much an urban junket within sight of skyscrapers as a stroll through the woods. In fact, the recent winters have lured so many cross-country skiers into the metropolitan parks of Chicago, New York, Boston, Montreal, and Detroit that converted roller skating concessions and golf shops can barely keep pace with the demand for cross-country rental gear.

Minneapolis and Toronto have zoos you can visit on skis. Minneapolis also has a city park within skiing distance of downtown that boasts two kilometers of night-lit ski trails covered with man-made snow. Since cross country imposes no dress codes, there is no one at any such places to force you to change out of coat and tie if you'd like to log a few K's on the way home from work.

Of course, classic cross country is more than just hearty exercise for the work weary. It's time with family and friends—far from the madding crowds —at a remote upcountry ski lodge. It's making Telemark runs off glaciers in the Pacific Northwest. It's a wine and cheese picnic. It's up to you to make it what you want.

GETTING STARTED

When winter snow and ice make jogging too slippery, ski touring is a natural replacement. The feeling of traveling almost effortlessly over the snow is thoroughly addictive. Many skiers I know now consider running as nothing more than "maintenance" training for skiing—to get them through the summer or the work week when they can't ski. This sport owes no allegiance to backpacking either. If you want, cross country *can* be as vigorous as lugging a fifty-pound pack for a week-long trek on the continental divide, *or* as leisurely as bird-watching and following animal tracks on a bright spring day.

Is it hard to do? Not if you transfer a slightly bent-over shuffling style to walking on skis. With today's convenient waxless models, you don't even have to wax the bottom of your skis. And you can get started in this sport without paying stiff membership fees, taking a bank loan, or trading your firstborn to the devil for trail tickets.

A decent introductory ski package—skis, poles, boots, bindings—can still be purchased for less than $150. You can ski in clothes you use for other winter activities. Trail fees at touring centers are one-third or less the price of downhill lift tickets. And if you still need a hedge against inflation, you can always ski near home. Snowed-over golf courses, summer hiking trails, river levees, bridle paths, logging roads, and our vast public lands are all potential ski trails to the imaginative skier, and access is free.

For beginning skiers, the following advice will get you off on the right foot:

1. Rent ski gear the first few times you go.
2. No need to ski alone. After all, cross country is a social sport. Go with friends who have skied before and will help make your first ski experience enjoyable.
3. Go to an established cross-country ski touring center that sets tracks so your first few strides will be a little less wobbly.
4. Take a lesson. The better you ski, the more fun you'll have.

WHO GOES CROSS-COUNTRY SKIING?

Everyone. This is a sport with universal appeal; it imposes no age limits, gender preferences, or physical barriers beyond the assurance of a physician that you are healthy.

- Slim, petite Carol Duffy was in her early forties when she caught cross-country fever. This Hayward, Wisconsin, housewife decided soon after the birth of her tenth child that she'd had enough of diapers and dishes. In 1972, she hired a babysitter once a week and started taking ski lessons at nearby Telemark Lodge. After only six days on cross-country skis, she was encouraged by an instructor to ski the 24-kilometer Korteloppet ski race at Telemark. Carol won the women's division of the race. Inspired by her success, Carol has been training for ski racing ever since. In 1980, she became the first person to complete all nine World Loppet international ski marathons (held in nine different nations) in the first two seasons the races were held as an organized league.
- John Day, a rancher from Medford, Oregon, didn't take up cross-country skiing until he was fifty-two. He was so smitten that shortly thereafter he announced his intention to make the 1964 Olympic Team! Although he never had the chance to try out, Day redirected his zeal toward the masters ski racing circuit (which he has been terrorizing for twenty years) and promoting cross-country skiing.

The Many Facets of Cross-Country Skiing

What is cross-country skiing? It's the annual skinny-ski invasion of Hayward, Wisconsin, during the American Birkebeiner ski marathon . . .

. . . or a spring tour in the high mountains with friends . . .

. . . or a leisurely cruise on machine-set tracks at a touring center.

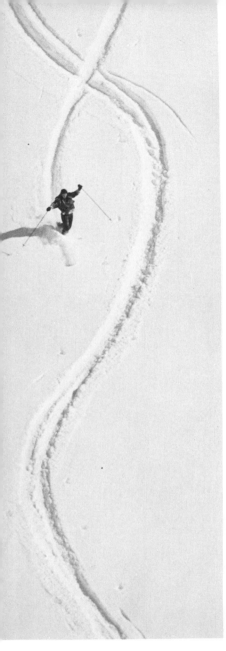

Even when the sun has fallen, the increasing number of illuminated trail systems in North America play host to night skiing, and to exciting night races such as this Dannon Series competition at Telemark Lodge, Wisconsin.

Cross-country skiing is also Telemarking! This graceful downhill turn—possible only on free-heel cross-country boot bindings—was revived by American skiers in the early seventies. Telemarking is popular both on groomed, lift-served slopes and in the deep snows of the backcountry .

Whether you choose bushwhacking through dense forests or effortless gliding through open meadows, cross-country skiing lets you go anywhere there is sufficient snow and in whatever direction your skis take you.

Day tours are cross-country skiing's winter counterpart to the day hike . . .

. . . and with a soft blanket of snow on the ground and the leaves off the trees, spotting wildlife and following animal tracks is easy.

Your only companions on
winter camping trips may
be solitude and beautiful
scenery . . .

. . . and backpacking in
winter on cross-country skis
lets you escape pesky
mosquitoes, black flies, and
summer backpacking
hordes.

· Jim Bando, twenty-nine, is a successful California sports photographer. He's carried a cherished dream with him since he first started skiing: to ski across California's Sierra. In 1982, Bando skied with two friends from Tioga Pass to Yosemite in twenty-four hours. "We didn't carry tents but had light sleeping bags with us in case we had to bivouac," recalls Bando. "That trip was the single most exhausting experience of my life, but one I'll never forget."

Everyone is taking up cross country. Former president Carter took a few well-publicized spins—and spills—on the trails at Camp David during his administration. Speed skater Beth Heiden traded thin blades for skinny skis and a spot on the University of Vermont ski team after the 1980 Winter Olympics. Marathon runners Frank Shorter, Bill Rodgers, and Gayle Barron are avid ski tourers. Every new skier you meet on the trail—whether speed-suited racer, smooth-striding senior citizen, or binocular-and-granola-laden woodsman— adds a fresh perspective and personality to this ancient sport.

FROM SCANDINAVIA TO THE SIERRA

Did skiing originate in the rolling hills of Norway and Sweden, or somewhere on the vast Siberian steppes? It depends on how you define "ski." A long slat with upraised tip? Made for supporting a skier sliding over snow?

Skis made out of bound-together grass reeds but closely resembling modern snowshoes have been found in the Altai Mountains of Siberia and carbon-dated to 2500 B.C. Skis made out of wood that look more like the skis we use now for touring were excavated many years ago from a Swedish peat bog. These skis and primitive rock wall drawings of a stick figure skier in Rodoy, Norway, also date back four thousand years.

The windows we peer through to trace the history of skiing provide memorable images. Early skiers didn't kick and glide across the land like modern skiers; they must have scootered. Finnish and Norwegian traveling skis were terribly mismatched: one ski was long and thin for gliding, the other short and wide with reindeer fur attached to the sole to provide purchase. Clearly, skiing was not so much recreation as lopsided kick-poling to cover the distances between villages. One hopes these early winter travelers switched skis frequently.

Eleventh- and twelfth-century Vikings used skis in battle. In fact, the original Norwegian Birkebeiner race commemorates the battle in which baby prince Haakon was carried to safety from Lillehammer to Rena, Norway, by two fur-clad, horn-helmeted Viking scouts. The distance between the two villages was 55 kilometers. ("Birkebeiner" means "birch-legs" in Norwegian, referring to the leggings worn by these soldiers to keep snow out of their moccasins.)

Skiing Comes to North America

When did cross-country skiing make its appearance on this continent? Harold Grinden, a ski historian from Duluth, Minnesota, holds the theory that the Vikings brought skiing to North America more than nine hundred years ago and that Leif Ericson's brother-in-law, Karlstenfi, who spent several winters on American shores, could not have endured the hard winters here without his slippery wooden boards.

Skis were certainly used in this country after the 1840s when Scandinavian immigrants fashioned wooden touring skis in the Midwest. Norwegian sailors who deserted ship in San Francisco to hunt gold in the Sierra brought skiing to California at the same time. To pass time in the winter, these Norwegians staged wild ski races at the mining camps, sometimes attaining speeds of 80

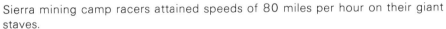

Sierra mining camp racers attained speeds of 80 miles per hour on their giant staves.

Snowshoe Thompson hauled the mail on skis from Placerville, California, to Carson Valley, Nevada, from 1856 to 1876.

miles an hour on heavy 20-foot planks. Bindings were simple leather straps, and ski bases were slickened with strange animal-vegetable essences such as spermaceti, tar, camphor, castor oil, and turpentine—the first ski waxes.

Many of these skiers slipped north to the Cascades while others crossed the desert to the Colorado mining camps when the California Gold Rush cooled down. One of the Norwegian immigrants who stuck around became a legend in the late nineteenth century in California—not as a downhill speed demon but as a long-distance, cross-country-skiing mailman. He was "Snowshoe" Thompson, the name given him for the 25-pound, 12-foot-long oak staves he wore in transporting the mail along a 90-mile route across the Sierra from 1856 to 1876.

The Modern Revival

Before 1830, the year when a fellow named Sondre Norheim invented a leg-scissoring, knee-bending turn for free-heel skiing in Norway, turning on cross-country skis had been a problem. Norheim's turn, invented in his home town, Telemark, was a great success at Norwegian ski festivals in the 1800s. More than a decade ago—about the same time cross-country skiing started to boom in this country—a handful of Rocky Mountain skiers rediscovered the Telemark turn and the great turning power it provides on both lift-served and backcountry slopes. The Telemark has brought new spirit, freedom, and controversy to cross-country skiing. Some see it as the reinvention of downhill skiing. Others view the Telemark as an American gift to the skiing world. Whatever . . . it works and it's fun.

Not to neglect the great contributions to skiing made by the millions of ski tourers who discovered cross country in the sixties and seventies, but several Americans also began to assert themselves on the international ski racing scene at the same time as cross-country skiing started taking off. John Bower ended the fifty-year dominance of nordic skiing competition by Scandinavians, Russians, and East Europeans by winning the King's Cup in the nordic combined (jumping and ski running) at the 1968 Holmenkollen Ski Festival. Then, at the 1976 Winter Olympics, a twenty-one-year-old Vermonter named Bill Koch stunned the world by taking a silver medal in the 30-kilometer race. To prove that an American winning a cross-country medal was no fluke, Koch demonstrated again that he was one of the world's premier skiers by taking the World Cup of cross-country skiing in 1982.

All this is to say that cross country has arrived in this country—as sport, as competition, and as fun. We've made great strides in developing our skiing, and as our competitive record shows, our skiers. But none of it would have been possible without the dedication of the following skiers.

Cross Country's Cast of Characters

No sport is without inspirational figures. Baseball has Ted Williams and Casey Stengel. Golf has Palmer and Nicklaus. Soccer has Pele. Cross-country skiing's heroes include:

John Caldwell. The father of American cross-country skiing, the witty, irreverent math teacher from Putney, Vermont, is credited with coaching more U.S. cross-country skiers to prominence than any other man, and with never losing sight of the fun that is as much a part of ski racing as the rigorous training needed to do well. The "Wizard of Putney" skied on the 1952 Olympic ski team, coached the U.S. team from 1966 to 1972, and authored the country's first ski touring texts.

Herman "Jackrabbit" Smith-Johannsen. If Caldwell is the father of American cross country, Jackrabbit is the grandfather of Canadian cross-country skiing. Born in Norway in 1875, the Jack-rabbit came to Canada in 1902 to work on the national railway. Still skiing at one hundred and seven years old, the Jackrabbit is proof of the old adage that "old skiers never die, they just shorten their strides."

Sixten Jernberg. The greatest cross-country ski competitor of all time, Jernberg is the Swedish logger and folk hero who trained in his work boots, swam through lakes instead of running around them, and ate up the competition between 1954 and 1964 in a pell-mell pursuit of four Olympic gold medals, three silvers, and two bronze.

Bill Koch. At twenty-eight years old, Koch is America's top cross-country racer. Koch started skiing at age three and actually skied to and from school each day as a child in Brattleboro, Vermont. A quiet, determined competitor, Koch has popularized a technique called *marathon skating* for long-distance racing on the flats, and he is considered one of the best downhill cross-country skiers in the world.

Ned Gillette. Leader of exotic ski adventures to remote mountain regions, Gillette, a former Olympic skier, developed a taste for wilderness skiing as director of the Yosemite Mountaineering and Trapp Family Lodge ski schools. Whether skiing around Mt. McKinley or Mt. Everest, or pulling heavy sleds across Ellesmere Island, Gillette has expanded the horizons of just what's possible to accomplish in this mobile, self-propelled sport.

Marty Hall. The tough, outspoken former U.S. team coach (1968–78) and present Canadian team coach, Hall resigned as U.S. coach after a power struggle between independent-thinking U.S. team skiers who had their own training ideas that were at odds with Hall's. Marty is a great boost to the Canadian program and stands firm in advocating closely supervised skiing, "specific" training, and total dedication to the sport.

HOW TO USE THIS BOOK

I doubt you'll carry this book with you in your day pack, so read it now from cover to cover. Then refer to it again—and again—when problems arise in your skiing. The text should serve as both inspiration and handy technical reference.

Obviously no book can substitute for practical experience, and there's something to be said for imitating better skiers, whether you see them in the pages of this book or watch them passing by on the trail. But there are no absolutes in skiing. What works for you is what's best. The final form is your own.

2

Gearing Up and Waxing

Not so long ago, any discussion of equipment and clothing for cross-country skiing would have been simple. Skis were wooden, poles were bamboo, boots made out of leather, and clothes fashioned from wool. Not today. . . . The revolution in petro-chemical technology has fostered fiberglass skis with convenient waxless running surfaces, light boron and graphite poles, waterproof plastic and Gore-Tex ski boots and clothing. In skis alone, industry changes in flex designs and waxless base configurations are coming on so fast you practically need a graduate degree in chemical engineering to stay informed.

Fortunately, the ski companies are dedicated to keeping things simple for the would-be confused consumer; the equipment makers traditionally have made four or five kinds of skis, boots, bindings, and poles corresponding to the different kinds of skiing in North America. The categories are *touring, light touring* (track skiing), *racing, mountaineering* (including lift-served Telemarking and backcountry skiing), and *children's skiing.* Many skiers will first purchase touring or light touring gear because of its versatility—it can be used on machine-groomed tracks *or* wilderness trails. Then you "graduate" at some point to

27

Waxing your skis correctly helps ensure a good day on the trail.

lighter or heavier equipment depending upon whether you like the performance characteristics of the lighter, faster gear or the heavier, more stable equipment. Or to put it another way, depending on whether you like to ski in or out of prepared tracks.

The intelligent way to thread through the equipment maze is to know what to look for. In this chapter we'll talk about testing skis in the ski shop so you can predict how they'll perform on snow. I'll point out important features in boots so you'll avoid buying the kind of low-quality footwear that will prevent you from having good control no matter which skis you buy. Finally, we'll discuss two other equipment matters that seem to give skiers problems: dressing correctly and selecting waxes.

WHICH SKI FOR YOU?

- *Touring* skis are wide and stable: a good choice for first-time skiers and those who ski off-trail most of the time. Most touring skis have polyethylene (P-Tex) plastic running surfaces, and the waxless models are patterned underfoot to give you grip on the snow without having to wax. Touring skis are sturdy and easy flexing for all but the heaviest skiers. And most have *sidecut,* which is the difference in width between tip, waist, and tail that gives the ski a slight hourglass appearance and makes the ski easier to turn.
- *Light touring* skis are lighter and thinner than touring skis (46 to 51 millimeters at the waist) for fast skiing on machine-set tracks. Most light touring skis have a livelier flex and stiffer camber (or curve) than touring skis; it takes a more emphatic down-push to set the wax or waxless pattern in the snow for grip. Light touring skis have parallel-cut (straight) sides, or minimal sidecut for frictionless gliding in tracks.
- *Racing* is to touring what running is to jogging—it's fast, demanding skiing on thin (44 to 46 millimeters) parallel-cut skis. Racing skis are the lightest skis made. Some of the new ones weigh only 650 grams apiece. That's lighter than an empty coffee mug! Racing skis have much stiffer cambers than touring skis, meaning a higher arch has been built into the ski to keep the midsection (and kick wax) from dragging in the snow when gliding down hills. Some racers carry two or three pairs of skis in their quiver: a stiffly cambered ski for wet snow conditions (a "klister ski"—named after the wax used in wet snow), a softer ski for powder snow (a "hard-wax ski"), and a waxless ski for those "zero-

A　　　　　　　　　　　　　　　　　　　　　　　**B**

An array of cross-country skis: (A) touring skis (left), waxless touring skis (middle), and thin superlight racing skis (right). Backcountry skis (B) range from wide edgeless models for deep snow (left), to sturdy metal-edged models for steep slopes and icy trails.

degree days" when the temperature hovers at the freezing point and selecting the right wax is nearly impossible.

· *Mountaineering* skis are virtually the same width as touring skis but sturdier. They have offset steel edges to facilitate downhill turning on steep slopes and provide extra security on icy trails.

· *Children's* skis should be waxless so their wearers can shuffle around and schuss tracks and jumps independent of Mom and Dad.

Waxable Versus Waxless

When you press down on the midsection of a cross-country ski, the camber flattens out and the base comes into contact with the snow surface. Here, under the foot, a ski either has a waxless pattern milled, stamped or otherwise implanted into the plastic running surface, or is smooth. Waxless patterns available now are the product of space-age technology. They come in a variety of designs from the newer hydrophilic chemical inserts, microscopic brushed-up polyethylene hairs, and temperature-sensitive rubber polymer and polyamide fiber compounds to the good old steps, scales, mica flakes, and mohair strips.

Understand, to get grip so you can walk or run on skis without slipping back, you must either apply wax to the ski base underfoot (called the "kick zone" or "wax pocket") or the ski's waxless pattern simulates the interaction

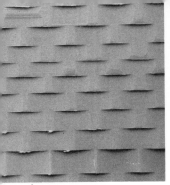

Steps and scales, or combinations of both, are but a few of the waxless patterns available that work like wax to provide grip *and* forward glide.

of wax and snow to hold the ski momentarily when you push down on it. Both waxable and waxless skis release their grips on the snow when you push forward in the glide.

Essentially, waxless skis work the same way as the fur-soled skis employed by the ancient Scandinavians. Just as you wouldn't pet the family hound in a direction opposite to the way his fur grows—without raising a few hackles, that is—so it is with waxless skis; the little backwards slanting protuberances allow the ski to slide forward but not slip back.

Waxless skis make sense if you ski frequently in an area where the temperature and snow conditions change a great deal. They're very convenient—no time-consuming, tricky waxing necessary. Just throw them in the back of the car, drive to the snow, put 'em on and go. Waxless skis work well in such areas as California, the Pacific Northwest, southern New England, the maritime provinces of Canada, southern Ontario, and coastal British Columbia and Alaska. In the Rockies and upper Midwest, where winter temperatures are relatively constant (calling for easy-to-apply hard waxes most of the time), waxable skis are preferred. But I'll let you decide for yourself which skis best suit your purposes:

PROS

Waxless skis: Work well in wet and rapidly changing snow conditions
Work well when the temperature hangs near the freezing point
Outperform badly waxed skis
Are convenient; you don't need to lug a waxing kit or use messy klister

CONS

Waxless skis: Sound like snow tires running on dry pavement
May glide poorly
Are not proven performers in icy snow or deep powder
May wear out after a couple of seasons of heavy use
Can't match the performance of well-waxed skis

Testing the Flex

In the ski shop, take a pair of skis off the rack and press the bases together with your hands. Can you squeeze the bases together easily or is there a gap you can't quite close? This is camber. If you place the skis right side up on the floor, the

Anatomy of a cross-country ski.

SIDECUT, CAMBER AND KICK ZONE

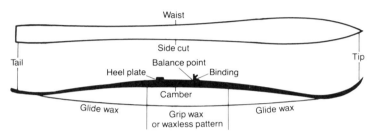

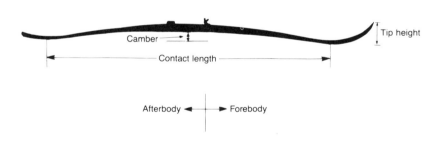

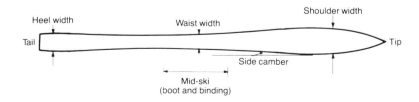

Hand-squeeze the bases of new skis against one another to get a subjective feeling for camber stiffness (left). Then check them to see that they match without warping or tip splay. Are they equally stiff?

midsection of each ski will arch upward. To get a feeling of how camber stiffness varies among skis, press together the bases of three or four sets of different kinds of skis—touring, light touring, racing, and metal-edged mountaineering. Can you discern any differences?

When hand-squeezing skis for camber, be aware that excessively soft skis will turn easily but glide poorly. A too-stiff ski will slip backwards on hills, be difficult to turn, and wear you out over the course of a long tour or race. Always look for skis with a moderate amount of camber. The trick is to select a ski that closely matches your weight and skiing ability.

Accomplished skiers can normally flatten a ski that takes two-thirds to all of their body weight to compress because they have the ability to make a near-total weight transfer during the kick. Good skiers avoid excessively soft skis because the skis will "belly out" in the glide. The strongest Olympic-caliber skiers may press up to three times their body weight in the kick, but they would never choose skis *that* stiff. Most of us should look for skis with cambers that compress at ten to forty pounds below body weight until we've developed the powerful mule kicks of the racers. Not sure which ski stiffness is for you? Then seek the advice of a knowledgeable shop salesperson or try one of the following tests:

The Paper Test

Light tourers and racers like to pick skis on their own and will often make use of the paper test to select skis of the right camber. To perform this test, place a pair of skis four to six inches apart on a *very flat surface*. You should stand where your feet will be when bindings are mounted—toes just forward of the balance point. Distribute your weight over the skis as evenly as possible.

Have a partner slide a piece of paper under the middle of the ski to see how much of the kick zone will be off the snow during the glide. Ideally, you should be able to slide the paper a total distance of about two and a half feet. If the paper is pinned to the floor, the skis are too soft. The skis are too stiff if you can slide the paper more than two and a half feet.

In well-constructed skis, your partner should be sliding the paper through a kick zone that starts just behind the heel of your foot and extends forward from that point the desired two to three feet. Warning: the paper test is unreliable with waxless skis. The paper will get caught on the ridges of "positive profile" base patterns, the kind that rise—like roof shingles—instead of recede from the level surface of the ski bottom.

The Paper Test: stand with weight evenly distributed over both skis while a partner slides a sheet of paper underneath your feet to determine the length of kick zone. Many ski shops match skis to your weight and skiing ability with a clamp-type pressure gauge (right).

Testing Camber with a Pressure Gauge

Many ski shops now have clamp pressure gauges such as the PSI Skeetester that customers can use to get a more accurate reading of camber than they can through hand squeezing or the paper test. To use the PSI or similar devices, put a pair of skis base to base and clamp them together an inch below the balance point. This is the point on the ski where you will push down with the ball of the foot during the kick. Screw the clamp in until the bases are less than a half-inch apart, but not so close that you can't see a gap between the skis.

The gauge will now read how many pounds of pressure were required to flatten the camber.

Tip Flex and Twist

To test a ski's forebody torque, grab the ski with one hand in the midsection, and with the other hand twist the ski tip—actually try to rotate it as though you were unscrewing a jar—to see how stiff it is torsionally. If the tip is stiff, the ski will hold an edge well in icy conditions. If soft, it is better suited for powder snow and crud. A torsionally soft light touring or racing ski will ride smoothly through track-set corners.

Next, pull the ski tip *straight back toward you* and push the midsection away as though flexing a bow. (The ski's tail should be resting on the floor with the running surface facing away from you.) Does the front half of the ski, including the tip and forebody, hinge easily and smoothly? Sample several skis

Twisting the tips tests for torsional rigidity (left), while the hinge test measures how far and how smoothly the forebody flexes into the middle of the ski.

in this manner and you'll have an idea how the different skis will perform when riding over bumps and depressions in the snow. Generally, a ski with a stiff forebody will be more stable and straight running than a ski with a softer tip. Soft-tipped skis ride smoothly over bumps and dips, and float well in soft snow.

Length

Buy skis in the normal floor-to-wrist length unless you do a lot of cross-country downhilling or can't find a racing/training ski soft enough for your weight. *Then* consider a ski five centimeters shorter than normal. Nordic downhillers will be able to swivel shorter skis a little more easily; women—and others light for their height—can use slightly shorter skis with no adverse effect on ski performance.

A word to deep-powder Telemarkers. Remember those delicious knee-deep days of seasons past? You may sacrifice flotation with shorter skis. In deep powder, many western backcountry skiers use skis 215 to 230 centimeters long —almost as long as the giant staves Snowshoe Thompson wore to carry the mail across the Sierra in the 1850s.

Normally, buy skis that reach from the floor to your upstretched wrist, but also consider your weight and skiing ability.

THE RIGHT BOOTS AND BINDINGS

Good boots are critical to your enjoyment of skiing. Don't make the mistake of spending a bundle on skis and leaving yourself short when it comes to boots. You'd be better off buying higher-quality, expensive boots first. You won't be able to turn those skis if you buy the kind of poorly made, torsionally soft boot that can be twisted in your hands like a towel.

When a cross-country ski is turned or pivoted, the force is transmitted at a point a couple of inches behind the binding. Since the heel is not locked down in cross-country bindings, there is a tendency for the boot to slide laterally off the heel plate. Soft boots slide off the heel plate easily; stiff boots transmit turning power directly to the ski.

How can you tell which boots are torsionally rigid? In the hiking-shoe style of backcountry and Telemark boots, look for leather uppers, stitched Norwegian welts with metal or wood shanks, and sturdy Vibram lug soles. The best light touring and racing boots look like running shoes except for their lightweight, forward-flexible yet torsionally rigid nylon (Hytrel) soles.

Bindings are the link between boot and ski; bindings should be compatible not only with the boots you have but with the skis you buy. Touring and mountaineering skiers normally use bindings that are 75 millimeters wide at the point where the boot's stubby toe projection nestles into the three pin holes on the binding plate and is clamped down with a metal bail (hence their name "rat-trap bindings"). The wide 75-millimeter binding suits the purposes of wide touring and backcountry skis quite well.

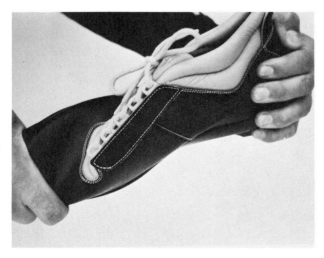

Avoid buying boots that you can twist in your hands like a wet dishrag.

Light touring and racing boot/binding systems are proliferating at a fantastic rate. The major differences between the most popular systems are in the width of the projecting boot sole, the matching binding width, the types of sole and heel stabilizing ridges employed, the thickness of the boot soles, and the way the boot secures itself to the binding. Presently we have 38-millimeter, 50-millimeter (with 7- or 12-millimeter sole thicknesses), and specialized boot/binding systems like Dynafit LIN and Salomon that incorporate linkage systems that work with no other boots or bindings but their own. Seems like there are a number of different ways to build a better rat trap.

It will surely work, but it doesn't make much sense to combine a 75-millimeter boot and binding with a racing ski. The boots and bindings weigh so much they completely defeat the purpose of having thin, light skis. Likewise, the narrow running boots are too cold and not sturdy enough for off-track treks.

75, 50, or 38?

The numbers are: (a) John Elway signaling a post pattern from the line of scrimmage, (b) the measurements of an expectant gorilla, (c) the confusing array of numbers that today's cross-country equipment buyer faces in trying to select the right boots and bindings for the skiing he will do.

If you chose c, you're probably wondering what the differences are between the narrow boot/binding systems like the 50s, 38s, Dynafit LIN, Salomon and (recently introduced) Nike boot/bindings and the traditional 75-millimeter stubby-toed touring boot. Aside from being 30 to 50 percent lighter than 75-millimeter bindings, the 38s, 50s and other special boot/bindings are almost one and a half inches narrower where the boot's toe projection is clamped to the binding. The narrower profile allows the boot and binding to slide faster in tracks because there is less surface friction against track sidewalls. If you've ever toured in cold, firm tracks and had the annoying experience of being tripped up by a piece of snow projecting onto the track, you know half the reasoning behind the development of the narrow-profile boot/bindings.

The other half is that the narrow boots have thinner soles that allow easy forward flexing of the boot in the stride; you can lift your foot up to perpendicular without the painful creasing across the toes common with 75-millimeter boots. Plus, the trailing ski stays flatter on the snow, so the danger of driving a ski tip into the track is greatly reduced. All this because the forward flex of the narrow-profile boots takes place on the sole projection between the binding and the ski, and not over the top of the foot.

There are a few drawbacks to the narrow-profile boots, however. Most are low cut and about as amply insulated as jogging shoes. Furthermore, the nylon

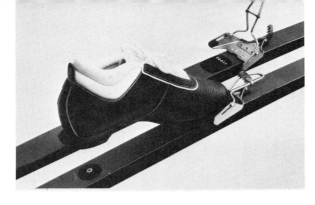

Boots

A low-cut 75-millimeter boot with compatible "rattrap" three-pin binding.

Narrow 50-millimeter bindings, ideal for racing boots, slide easily through tracks without getting caught on the sidewalls.

Noncompatible boot binding designs, that is, those that don't fit existing 75-, 50-, and 38-millimeter systems, change yearly to the benefit of light tourers and racers.

Sturdy, lug-soled boots and beefy 75-millimeter bindings are made for Telemarking and off-track touring.

(Hytrel) boot soles on 50/7, 38-millimeter, and Salomon boots are thin, providing little insulation for the bottom of the feet. Wearers sometimes complain that the nylon soles are slippery to walk on (despite manufacturers' recent efforts to implant rubber pads for traction) and that they need to wear overboots or add foam insoles in cold weather.

For some skiers, the solution may be the 12-millimeter-thick sole available on some 50-millimeter-wide boots. These boots have the binding width of the 50/7 racing boots but the sole thickness (12 millimeters) of 75-millimeter touring boots. But if you do a lot of skis-off scrambling over rocky terrain or need to kick steps in steep snow on mountain tours, you'll prefer the surefootedness of 75-millimeter lug-soled backcountry boots.

High or Low Cut?

Whatever you may have heard, high-cut boots don't make it much easier for you to control your skis. Building up your ankle strength in the off-season and developing good ski technique are far more important factors. But high-cut boots do keep the snow out of your socks. So if you already own a pair of stiff, low- or medium-cut boots, simply add an overboot or gaiters on off-trail trips.

Good Fit

Two kinds of fit—a tight link between boot and binding and comfortable fit between foot and boot—are very important. In choosing backcountry boots (75 millimeters), allow plenty of room for socks and a half-inch at the toe so blood can circulate freely and toes don't get pinched on long tours. Since the forward flex on narrow-profile boots takes place on the extended sole, these boots can be fitted more like running shoes. Allow a quarter-inch of wiggling space in the toe, but make sure the heel fits snugly so it won't blister.

Select bindings that clamp the toe of the boot down securely and don't allow any side-to-side fishtailing that will quickly wear down the boot toe and reduce control over the ski.

Heel Devices

They have a variety of names: cones, prongs, wedges, ridges, keels, poppers, and locaters. They serve to keep the boot heel from slipping off the ski during turns by stabilizing the boot under the ball of the foot or at the heel. Many of the

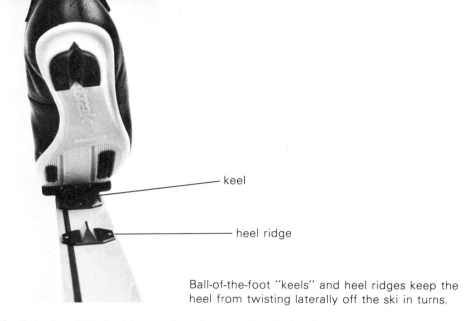

keel

heel ridge

Ball-of-the-foot "keels" and heel ridges keep the heel from twisting laterally off the ski in turns.

heel devices fitted with metal teeth serve the dual role of reducing snow build-up under foot.

Ball-of-the-foot stabilized boot/bindings, in contrast to heel stabilizers, hold the foot at a point where there is less lateral torque. On snow, you'll notice better control because your foot stays centered on the ski through 80 percent of the kick cycle as well as in maneuvers like skating (see page 68) and herringboning (page 80). Your foot is firmly rooted to the ski even when raised as much as 30 degrees off the top of the ski.

Heel locaters are the plastic spur devices that extend from the heel of boots and fit into a V-shaped wedge behind the heel to keep boots centered on the ski when the heel is down during turns. Some models can be locked down, but most allow the boot to lift freely in a vertical direction for diagonal striding. The advantage of heel locaters is that they add torsional rigidity to soft boots —especially those with molded rubber soles—and reduce stress on 75- and 50-millimeter boots' pin holes by relieving lateral tension on the boot toe.

If you have a stiff and secure boot/binding combination with no side play, you don't need heel locaters. They won't help you turn any better, and they may increase the danger of ankle injuries in slow, twisting falls.

PICKING PROPER POLES

Skiers skied with only one ski pole a hundred years ago. They used it for braking. In 1887, skiers started using two poles, and, as cross-country technique has evolved since that time, we have come to rely on poles to provide 25 percent of forward propulsion down the trail. Now that we're agreed that poles are important, it's only a matter of determining which shaft materials, grip designs, and basket shapes best suit the conditions you ski in most.

Tourers need flexible, durable poles that won't break easily. Tonkin cane and fiberglass are inexpensive and strong. Light tourers prefer lighter, stiffer poles of aluminum, fiberglass, or carbonfiber that translate arm and shoulder power efficiently during track skiing. Racers seek out the lightest carbonfiber and boron poles for the low swing weights, high strength-to-weight ratios, aerodynamic rake or V-shaped basket designs, and sharp carbide steel tips for easy pole planting on groomed trails.

Backcountry poles should be stronger and have wider baskets than the poles you'd use for track skiing. Fiberglass and cane are good choices, but aluminum is often preferred because it can be bent back into a semblance of its original shape if fallen upon. Wide, round baskets—throwback designs to the thirties and forties—are also excellent because they support a pole planted in deep snow.

Grips? The materials don't matter too much. Leather grips feel warmer to the touch than plastic. But plastic can be good because it doesn't soak up as much water as leather during a long tour. One feature in poles is crucial, however: adjustable wrist straps. Whether you buy poles with leather or nylon straps, make sure there is some kind of buckle adjustment to tighten the straps.

Select pole baskets that match the skiing you do: wide, round baskets for off-track (A, B), rake and butterfly for in-track skiing (C, D) or compromise shape (E) for both.

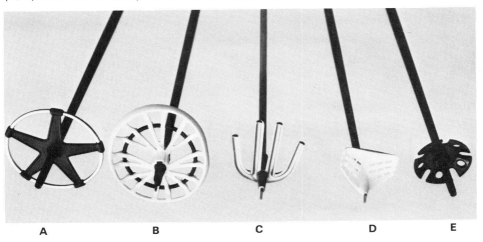

A   B   C   D   E

Poles should reach from the snow to your armpit when your arm is outstretched.

Otherwise, you'll be hammer-locking the pole grips during the poling follow-through for fear of throwing the poles away.

For touring and racing, *buy poles in the floor-to-armpit length.* Backpackers and Telemarkers will often use poles 5 to 10 centimeters shorter than normal to get better pole plants in downhill turning and because skiing with a heavy pack restricts your reach. Instead of buying shorter poles, or choking up on the poles you have for downhilling, you might consider getting one of the variable-length aluminum poles (such as those made by Alpine Research) that can be telescoped from cross-country to alpine length in seconds.

Another aluminum pole that makes a lot of sense for backcountry travel is the Life-Link avalanche probe pole. These poles can be joined together, and, in the event that a companion is buried in an avalanche, the double-length pole can be used to probe the snow to locate the victim.

DRESSING FOR CROSS-COUNTRY SKIING

Donning the right duds for cross country can be as simple as sliding into a suggestively tight one-piece suit or as calculating as adding moisture transport layers to a mountaineering ensemble you could wear in a snow cave at 20 below zero. Most simply, the clothes you wear depend on how fast you ski and the weather you will encounter.

Most beginning ski tourers make the mistake of overdressing for the occasion. Bulky wool pants, quilted snowmobile suits, and knee-length ski parkas are fine for the post-ski wrap-up, but far too restrictive and hot for energetic skiing. Another mistake first-timers make is wearing the wrong kinds of clothing. Blue jeans and cotton long johns are fashionable and comfortable wear around town, but serve no functional purpose on the trail. They get wet easily and stay wet.

Whether clad in classic knickers, turtleneck, and weatherproof top, or in a sleek and stretchy one- or two-piece nylon suit, the modern cross-country skier has chosen clothing that performs most of the following functions:

1. It provides protection from the environment.
2. It allows moisture and heat generated by vigorous skiing to dissipate rapidly.
3. It is comfortable to move in.
4. It allows the skier to vary the amount of insulation.

Keeping warm and dry—and trying to maintain a stable body temperature —while exercising at a fast pace is no simple matter. The key is to wear a nonmoisture-absorbing layer next to the skin. The new hydrophobic polypropylene underwear is a good choice because the polypropylene plastic thread (the same material that is woven into water ski rope and disposable baby diapers) does not retain moisture, so heated perspiration passes right through to the next layer. This middle layer—possibly a thin insulative covering such as a light wool turtleneck—should create "dead air space" to hold warm air close to the body.

Active skiers need only one more layer: either a one-piece bib knicker or two-piece knicker suit of comfortable wind-resistant fabric. Less active tourers can increase the amount of insulation they wear with a wool shirt, pile bunting jacket or down vest, and in wet or windy weather, a protective anorak. There are as many solutions to the puzzle of dressing correctly for cross country as there are styles of clothing available to make you look good doing it. Over the years, I've learned that the following rules apply for safe, comfortable dressing:

- *Avoid cotton clothing.* Although comfortable, cotton underwear, corduroy knickers, and poplin shells absorb water easily and hold it. Old standbys such as wool and the newer synthetics, fiberpile and polypropylene, stay warm even when wet.
- *Wear knickers.* Long pants legs rub together continually on a long tour; the constant chafing can be a pain especially if the pants are made of a heavy material. The only exceptions to the knickers-only rule are light warm-up pants and one-piece racing suits.
- *Knickers and bib knickers with material extending higher on the back*

Dressed for every ski situation (from left): the touring look, sleek track and racing outfits, functional backcountry wear.

will protect the lower back and kidneys and keep snow out of your britches in falls.

· *Don't hesitate to ventilate* at the first sign of overheating. In cold weather, wet clothes are dangerous. Dry equals warm. Knicker tops with full front zippers can be vented in seconds if you start to sweat. But zip up before you chill.

· In my opinion, the breathable yet waterproof wonder fabrics like *Gore-Tex and Klimate are highly overrated.* Just as good a protective outer layer in nasty weather is waterproof nylon. Far less expensive too. Surprisingly, the tightly woven nylon stretch fabrics in today's one- and two-piece suits are quite breatheable and yet snow repellent enough for day tours.

· *Look for tops with large collars* that can be turned up to deflect wind.

Hats, Masks, and Earmuffs

Trying to keep your body warm without wearing a hat is like trying to keep the house heated in winter after the roof has caved in. Keep your head covered to trap the 70 percent of body heat that normally escapes through the surface capillaries of your neck and noggin. If you start to overheat, take your hat off for a few minutes to cool down.

If wool hats make your forehead feel like it's crawling with ants, then try one of the polypropylene-lined nylon hats or racing headbands. In extremely cold weather, a leather face mask will prevent frostbitten cheeks. Racers are often seen wearing light, disposable Dr. Kildare surgical masks when even the mercury at the bottom of the thermometer is shivering. The white fabric masks can be purchased at medical supply stores.

To top off your cold weather cover-up, you might try a pair of the lightweight earmuffs that have been the rage on the racing scene ever since Bill Koch first modeled them in cold-weather competitions a few years ago. Wear them with or without a hat.

Gloves and Socks

You can lose another 15 percent of body heat from your hands and feet. Doesn't it seem that hands and feet are the first to get cold and the hardest to keep warm? The reason is that the body would rather keep its central core warm than circulate blood out to the extremities.

Number one strategy for keeping hands and feet toasty? Again . . . wear a hat! Number two strategy: the right gloves and socks. As with other clothing, the thickness of hand protection varies from light leather handball-type gloves that don't interfere with the poling motion to bulky expedition mitts whose major virtue is the freedom and warmth they allow your fingers by letting them rub against one another. Foot coverings range from light nylon and polypropylene socks to heavier wool and fiberpile—in ankle to knicker-high lengths.

The layering principle also applies to hands and feet. Backcountry skiers often combine Dachstein wool or fiberpile mitts with a nylon or Gore-Tex overmitt. Tourers can use a space liner or silk glove inside leather gloves on cold days. The inner gloves are also great for handling cameras, waxing torches, and stoves.

Two layers of socks work best on feet: an inner sock of moisture-dissipating material and a warm insulating outer sock. In the coldest weather, many skiers make use of the *vapor barrier effect* to keep their feet warm. A plastic bag—grocery store vegetable or freezer bags are suitable—slipped over the foot before the first sock layer will hold perspiration next to the foot so it doesn't get outside sock layers wet.

Overboots and Gaiters

Like the original birch-bark leggings worn by Scandinavian warriors a thousand years ago, gaiters keep snow off knicker socks and out of boots. The best gaiters cover the calves (they can be turned down in warm spring skiing) and fit snugly over the top of the boot. Gaiters that zip up the side of the leg are the most convenient and snowproof. Look for models that have a snap-flap over the bottom of the zipper to keep snow from freezing in the zipper. (Trying to remove gaiters by melting the snow off with a torch is a bit harmful to plastic zippers, not to mention the nylon or Gore-Tex fabric!)

There are also some nifty new Thinsulate and fiberpile-backed overboots on the market for racers and light tourers. The low overboots are designed for use with the low-cut, thinly insulated running-style boots that always seem to get wet or cold. The new overboots are much more durable than the old-style rubber overboots.

HOW WAX AND SNOW INTERACT

The first ski waxes were used by the California gold miners in the 1850s. To make their 12-foot staves slide faster, the miners whipped up fragrant concoctions of spermaceti, pine pitch, and castor oil. Great for the down-runs, but the miner-racers still had to use fur climbing skins to get back to the top. We now have petrochemical-based waxes that provide fast glide for sliding and grip for the hills and are as reliable as climbing skins. How is this possible? To understand how wax works, we need to shrink down to snowflake size and have a look at the underside of a cross-country ski.

Snowflakes carry their soft, pointy, and classically crystalline appearance until they sit on the ground too long or get warmed by the sun. Like people, snowflakes become round and lumpy with age. When you push down (actually apply weight) on the midsection of a properly waxed ski, the little icy points of the snowflakes push into the wax and hold the ski for a moment. This wax-snow bonding is broken when the ski is pushed forward in the glide. Thereupon the ski actually slides on a microscopic layer of water melted by the friction of ski rubbing against snow.

How wax works.

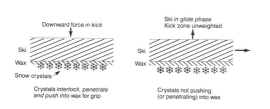

Thus, waxing is the art of matching the right wax to the prevailing temperature and snow conditions. There are two kinds of wax for the grip or kick zones of your skis: *hard wax* in tin canisters for *soft new snow* and *klister wax* in toothpastelike tubes (because klister wax is soft and gooey) for *old snow*—that is, snow that has thawed and refrozen several times.

The glide zones of skis also need to be waxed so that the tips and tails will slide easily. Here you need to apply a hard paraffinlike wax that will not only protect the ski base from drying out but improve its performance as well. To choose the right wax for the day's skiing you need (1) to check a thermometer to determine the air temperature, (2) test the snow conditions present, then (3) combine these two bits of information with the aid of a wax chart or the printed descriptions of temperature and snow conditions on wax tins.

Reading the Snow

They say an Irishman can distinguish fifty shades of green and that Eskimos have hundreds of names for snow. Luckily, cross-country waxes cover such a broad range of temperatures and snow types that we don't need to be nearly as discerning as the Eskimos or the Irish. Such discernment can help, however, especially on those nasty waxing days when intuition and experience may prove far more useful than a forty-pound wax box full of snow thermometers, humidity-detecting hygroscopes, and fifty narrow-temperature-range waxes.

It takes practice to match grip and glide waxes to the day's snow conditions. And there are days when you'll resort to flipping a coin. The first step in reading the snow is to check the air temperature with a thermometer. Then

Make a snowball to check snow for moisture content before selecting the correct grip wax.

check the snow type by making a snowball. Freshly fallen or unmelted snow crumbles in your hands. Wet snow packs easily into Koufax-style hardballs.

Whatever the snow conditions, *the colder the air temperature, the harder the wax or klister* you'll apply to the midsection of your skis. From very cold to warm air temperatures, hard-wax colors range from polar (clear), green, blue, violet (just below freezing), to red and yellow (above freezing).

The klisters follow virtually the same color spectrum from cold to warm: green, blue, violet (below freezing), to red, silver, and yellow. The klisters are designed to be used in the same air temperatures as the like-colored hard waxes, but in different snow conditions. You may have noticed that cold snow waxes have cold colors and warm snow waxes come in warm colors. This color scheme is relatively standard within the many brands of wax available in this country.

The simplified two-wax systems take the mystery out of waxing: one can for wet snow, one for dry.

Beginners can take most of the mystery out of waxing by learning to wax with one of the simplified two-wax systems currently available. The two waxes, one for dry snow, one for wet snow, provide grip in a wide range of temperature and snow conditions. To use these waxes, take note of the air temperature and snow conditions. Is the snow dry and soft? Does it blow away in the wind? Or is it mushy and wet? In the Swix two-wax system, for example, gold wax works in dry snow, silver works in wet snow.

As you become familiar with the two waxes, you can start to add waxes from the full spectrum of choices. This is the gradual approach to learning to judge waxing conditions correctly and will quickly give you the confidence to experiment as daringly as the "wax scientists" who seem to spend hours putting the finishing touches on a wax job.

Applying Grip Wax

Hard waxes are easy to apply. Simply peel back the leaded tin container to expose the stick of wax, then crayon a uniform, thin layer to the bottom of the ski underfoot from a point just behind the heel plate forward about two and

Crayon grip wax in a thin layer to the midsection of the ski base from just behind the heel plate forward two and a half feet. Then smooth with a synthetic or natural cork. Olympic biathlete, Peter Karns (right), touches up a wax job on the trail without taking off skis. Note the length and position of his kick wax.

a half feet. If the wax doesn't rub on easily, try heating it with a torch at the point where the wax emerges from the tin. Smooth the wax with a cork, set the skis outside for a few moments to cool, and go skiing.

If, after a hundred yards or so, the skis start to slip, stop and apply a thicker layer of wax. If that doesn't work, make a longer kick zone by waxing farther toward the tip of the ski. Skis still slipping? Apply a thin layer of the next softer wax over the first layer.

Klister

The person who coined the phrase "whole 'nother ball of wax" was probably talking about klister. Klister is messy, sticky stuff, and skiers often go to amazing lengths to avoid using it. I've witnessed skiers applying half-inch-thick

Gooey klister should be squeezed on both sides of the base groove in squiggly lines, then spread into a thin uniform layer with a plastic spreader.

A torch makes klister spread more easily outdoors. This skier has applied klister in "tractor treads"—also a good technique for mixing klisters before smoothing it out.

gobs of hard wax, cutting notches with a knife into the P-Tex base of their skis —anything to keep klister from attaching itself like some alien ooze to hands, hair, and clothing.

But klister is necessary, although evil. Any time the snow is old and granular (a condition often prevalent in the reconstituted snow of machine-set tracks), you have to use it to keep your skis from slipping back.

If you can, apply klister indoors, especially if you don't have a torch to heat up the wax tube so the wax will flow more quickly. Squeeze a thin line of klister on each side of the base groove of the ski. You can also make horizontal "tractor treads" and smooth the klister with the plastic spreader that comes standard with every klister box.

With klister, less is more: apply the stuff in very thin layers. A couple of blasts from a waxing torch will speed the spreading process. A hand-held iron heated with a torch or an ordinary household iron set on the lowest setting can also be used to heat both klisters and hard waxes and smooth them onto the ski. Once you've scraped the excess wax out of the sidewalls and grooves and set the skis outside to cool off, you're ready to go. Forget to cool your skis before you stride off, though, and you'll likely melt the top layer of snow onto the bottom of your skis: a frustrating experience to say the least.

A word about kicker lengths—i.e., the length of grip wax on the ski's midsection—and a warning about using torches and irons. Klister kickers are shorter than hard-wax kickers. I've seen some skiers get away with kickers little more than a foot long, but they had powerful enough technique to get away with it. Compared to hard-wax kickers, klister kickers can be from six inches to a foot shorter depending on how your ski's camber pocket is shaped.

Now to torches and irons. Warning: Too high heat will close the plastic micropores on polyethylene ski bases, effectively ruining the ski's wax-retentive properties. Keep heat settings low; keep torches moving quickly over the ski. The wax should never get so hot that it smokes.

The Importance of Binders

Also called base waxes, binders are durable synthetic rubber compounds used to hold klister wax to the ski in cold, abrasive snow (namely, most cold-weather klister snow). A binder is the first of two layers of wax and is applied underneath klister.

Binders are available in spray form or are packaged in familiar wax tins. Spray binders are sprayed into the kick zone and allowed to dry and harden. Tin-type binders should be rubbed or ironed onto the ski base, then smoothed. Scrape the groove and sidewalls clean. After the ski has cooled and the binder is hard, polish the binder with a cork. (Don't use this cork for polishing hard waxes, as binder screws up the kick and glide capabilities of hard wax.) Apply the klister right over the top of the binder when it is cool and smooth. Binder makes klister last almost twice as long as normal.

To prepare new skis, wrap fine-grain sandpaper around a square block and sand from tip to tail to smooth the P-Tex ruff (A). Then, with an iron on low setting, drip melted paraffin into tip and tail zones of your skis to protect the base and improve glide (B). Iron glide wax into the ski bottom to saturate P-Tex micropores. Keep iron

A	B	C

"But I thought my skis were ready to go as soon as I took them out of the shop!" you say. Maybe they were—if shop personnel sanded the base of the skis to remove the P-Tex ruff, flushed the base clean, then sealed the polyethylene micropores with paraffin or color-coded glide wax. Fiberglass skis—especially racing and light touring models—must be hot-waxed when they are new to protect the base from drying out and "glide waxed" to make the tips and tails ride faster. Glide-waxed skis also last longer and hold wax better.

To prepare new skis for hot waxing, pick up a selection of #120 to #170 sandpapers. Get the kind that can be used wet or dry on wood or plastic. Wrap the largest-grit paper around a square sanding block. Place the the skis bottom-up on a stable bench and sand with easy strokes, *always pushing from tip to tail* to keep the P-Tex hairs facing backwards. Sand the groove as well. Gradually move to lighter-grit sandpapers until the base is smooth. You don't need to sand the kick zones.

Many skiers remove irregularities and smooth the base with a metal scraper. It will work just as well, as long as you use a scraper that will hold a straight edge. Again, scrape from tip to tail.

Next, flush the base with water to get rid of sanding residue. Dry the base with a clean towel or, better, a lint-free fiberlene rag. You can also flush the

moving so you don't melt the ski base (C). Scrape excess glide wax from tip to tail (D). When, using a softer red glide wax for warmer conditions, you can break up ski-slowing suction between wet snow and the ski base by striating the smoothed-in wax with a wire brush (E).

D

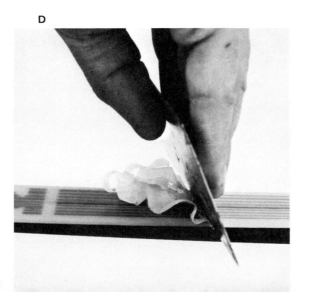

E

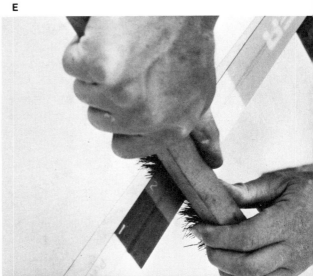

base with a liquid wax remover. Now your skis are ready for a paraffin-based glide wax or alpine speed wax suited for the snow conditions you most often ski in. Like the kick waxes, glide waxes are color-coded by hardness from green (the hardest) to blue, violet, and red.

In midwinter, I usually choose a violet glider wax, since it is a good mid-range wax and I rarely encounter severe cold weather where I ski. In spring, I'll wax my skis' tips and tails with a red glider because it has a high ratio of paraffin to hardening agent to make it more water repellent in wet snow. The harder green and blue waxes designed for cold-weather skiing have more of the hardening agent. You can use them in spring, but they will glide poorly. Don't like to keep switching gliders through the season? Try a universal glider suitable in all conditions. Whether you're a beginner or seasoned veteran, glide waxing makes sense because it takes more effort to push a bare ski a given distance than it does to push a ski that's been hot-waxed in the tips and tails. That's why glide waxing is also called "speed waxing."

Applying Glide Wax

Always apply glide wax in a warm room. Although cross-country glide waxes last longer than alpine speed waxes, racers claim the alpine waxes are a touch faster. Whichever wax you use on your skis, the application of both is the same.

You need an iron. If you use the household iron, don't plan on ironing another shirt with it—ever. With the iron on a low setting, hold the wax against the face of the iron so that the wax drips along either side of the groove in the tips and tails of your skis. Iron the wax droplets into the ski base with light, quick strokes. The iron is too hot if the wax smokes—and much too hot if the base starts smoking. When the wax has cooled for five or ten minutes, pull off the excess wax by scraping from tip to tail with a sharp *plastic* scraper. Clean the sidewalls and grooves with the edge of the scraper.

A minor point, but an important one for performance-minded skiers: When glide waxing for warm-weather skiing, the glide zones will be longer than they normally are for cold weather because klister kickers are shorter than hard-wax kickers.

Glide waxing regularly is very important in wet snow conditions to reduce the ski-slowing suction of mushy snow. When using warm-snow gliders, it is common to striate the glide zones with a brush to make tiny grooves that will reduce the amount of suction.

Finally, always seal the bases of your skis with glide wax before summer storage to protect them from excessive moisture, heat, or dryness.

What Went Wrong?

Missing the wax is as frustrating as watching the river boil with trout as your fly bobs downstream unscathed. You don't have what it takes! And now you're either dragging a couple of snow anchors from the bottom of your skis or slipping back desperately on every little incline. The solution? It's back to the waxing table for repairs, or time for a hastier on-snow adjustment. Here are a few solutions to some common waxing mishaps:

1. *Skis slipping?* The solution may be a thicker kicker. Then go longer (crayon more wax toward tips and tails) or, as a last resort, apply a softer wax right on top of the first layer.

2. *Skis won't move?* Only in rare situations can you apply hard wax over soft. Old waxing analogy: Would you spread peanut butter over jelly in making a sandwich? You could, but you wouldn't. If your skis won't move, scrape the soft wax off and apply a harder wax.

3. *What about hard wax over soft?* The first time I skied California's Echo Summit to Kirkwood race, there was a dusting of new snow covering consolidated corn snow—the infamous "dust over crust." The day promised to warm considerably, and the course had a 1,500-foot hill to be climbed in the first three miles. The wax? Red klister cooled in the shade until it became a rock-hard binder for a layer of hard red wax. By the time we skied through the soft new snow, temperatures rose dramatically and the klister kicked in and carried us over the hill. In breakable crust or light powder over crust, try a blue klister "cushion" for hard blue. Soft waxes under hard waxes make good binders.

4. *Transitional snow.* Normally, you should wax for the coldest snow you'll encounter on a tour. But when temperatures wobble about the freezing point, finding the right wax is a devilish task. One method that often works in these conditions is to keep adding progressively softer wax layers until you find one that works.

Keep your skis moving so the snow doesn't ball up underfoot. If they start to ice up, lift the ski up and give it a whack with your ski pole. Actually, a light tap will often do, and will keep you from splintering a nice pole. You can also

Stowe, Vermont's Bill Jaspersohn contemplates a less-than-perfect wax job that was suggested by the author. Time to scrape off old wax, replace with a harder wax, and shorten the kicker a bit.

Carry extra waxes, cork, scraper, dry gloves, and hat for long days on the trail.

rub the bottom of your skis over the top of a companion's skis. If all else fails, stop, scrape, and rewax.

5. *Tricky spring snows.* Try silver klister in pine-needle- and dirt-encrusted snow or if you'll be skiing in and out of the shade all day. Silver klister has metal particles in it that make it less tacky than other klisters.

Also try one of the universal klisters available that work in a broad range of granular snow conditions. Swix universal klister works from -5°C. to 10°C. —a very wide range indeed.

Removing Wax

Stripping wax off skis should be as thorough and regular a process as brushing your teeth. Do it every day you ski. With today's powerful liquid wax removers, the task of cleaning off wax has been greatly facilitated. But always wear rubber gloves or a plastic bag over your hands when using wax remover. I've seen faulty batches of the stuff that were so volatile that they melted holes in a plastic ski base!

The first step in wax removal is to scrape off as much wax as possible with a scraper. A torch and rag will speed the process. Dissolve the remaining wax with liquid solvent and allow the solvent to sit on the ski for thirty seconds. Then wipe the ski clean with a cloth. On snow camping trips, you can use white gas to clean ski bases if you have to switch waxes, although the gas may leave a slight residue that could impede good wax-to-ski bonding.

REPAIRING DAMAGED SKIS

Repairing rock-gouged ski bases is simple. Buy a P-Tex candle at the ski shop. Remove all wax from the area of the ski near the holes you want to fill. Make sure the base is dry and clean.

Light the P-Tex candle and drip the molten plastic into the scratches. Hold the candle no closer than three inches from the ski base so the plastic lava won't be too hot and melt the surrounding ski base when it hits the ski. Allow the filled-in area to cool, then scrape the surface smooth with a metal scraper to remove excess plastic.

Use P-Tex candles to fill gouges in the ski base. Then, scrape excess P-Tex so base is flush and smooth.

Delaminations to the tips and tails of skis can be filled with epoxy and set with C-clamps. Separate the exposed inside layers of the ski as wide as possible and fill with epoxy. Clamp the ski's topsheet and bottom together and wipe off the excess epoxy so it doesn't dry on the outside of the ski.

WAXLESS SKI CARE

Except that they need not be waxed for grip, waxless skis deserve the same treatment as waxable skis. The tips and tails should be glide waxed just as frequently as the glide zones on waxable skis. And to keep the waxless pattern from icing up in transitional snow conditions, try one of the currently available silicon or Teflon sprays.

SKINNY SKINS FOR CLIMBING

Imported from Europe where alpinists used them in long Haute Route crossings, mohair and polypropylene climbing skins—now available in slim 30-millimeter width for cross-country skis—have become essential to American backcountry skiers for climbing mountain passes and long slopes. The best ski skins attach to ski tips with a metal D-ring and cling to the bottom of the ski by means of a tacky adhesive called Coll-Tex.

With their grippy fur surfaces, climbing skins make mountains into molehills.

Skins make long mountain tours easier. When you're climbing two or three high passes a day with a heavy pack, it takes a lot less energy to stop once, put on climbing skins, and step smartly to the top than to stop and rewax five times as you gain elevation, as the temperature continues to drop, and as the snow conditions change. Another invention of the ancient Scandinavians applied in a new way. . . .

3

Skiing the Flats: Fundamentals

Enough talk about equipment and waxing. It's time to discuss the basic flatland maneuvers you'll use 75 percent of the time you go skiing. If you read only one chapter in this book, make this it. Diagonal striding and double poling are the two most important techniques in cross-country skiing. Learn them properly right from the beginning and you'll ski faster and with less effort.

Although striding and double poling are the first techniques cross-country skiers learn, for some reason they are the hardest to perfect. This chapter, and the three that follow, will introduce you to the fundamental moves that are the building blocks of advanced technique. Beginners will use this introductory material to rehearse the elementary maneuvers of cross-country skiing before their first outings. Advanced skiers can use the pictures and text to brush up on the basics and correct common mistakes before they become habits.

No book devoted to ski technique is a substitute for on-snow experience. Sound, basic instruction and practice will lead you down the path to solid technique; let this book serve as a trail marker to point you in the right direction. How quickly and effectively you acquire good ski tech-

61

Bill Koch displays the powerful striding motion that has made him one of the fastest cross-country skiers in the world.

nique is up to you. As Dick Taylor, the ski touring director at Crosscut Ranch, Montana, once said, "The beginner is the prince of his dreams, moving comfortably and gracefully on skis. His only task is to accept himself as a total resource and quietly let loose the natural movements within."

USING IMAGERY AND VIDEOTAPE

Anyone who has tried to cut back on such vices as overeating or smoking knows that mental imagery is a powerful psychological technique that can help break bad habits. Now athletes in many sports are using mental imagery techniques to improve skills and change habits. The trick is to picture yourself surmounting technique obstacles by actually performing basic maneuvers correctly in your head long before you must execute them on the field of play—or in the case of skiing, on a field of snow.

Thinking positively about cross-country skiing is the first step toward learning to do it correctly. In the 1970s, a Colorado State University psychologist, Dr. Richard Suinn, introduced mental imagery techniques to the U.S. cross-country ski team. Added to sound training and closely supervised coaching, the ski team improved its international standing dramatically. Former U.S. team coach Marty Hall is a strong advocate of mental imagery. His advice to skiers is: relax your mind and body, then imagine how you will look when correctly performing the basic maneuvers of cross-country skiing. The key is to become an impartial judge, to stand outside your body and watch yourself making improved technical moves. When you see yourself as Nikolai Zimjatov or Bill Koch, it's time to take the fantasy to the ski trail.

Of course, it's important to have a mental image of good skiing style in your head before you try to imitate it. The picture sequences in this book are the place to start. Then spend an hour sometime this winter watching and imitating an instructor. Check out the lead skiers at a citizen race. Never stop thinking about skiing like the world's best skiers. Finally, if your ski touring center provides such services, or you have the opportunity to enroll in a performance skiing workshop, it's great fun and incredibly instructive to have your technique videotaped and critiqued.

I'm not satisfied with the comparisons drawn between running and cross-country skiing. Superficially, they look similar—opposite arm, opposite leg moving back and forth in unison—but there are numerous physiological differences. If you took a handful of the world's best distance runners and had them ski in a 10-kilometer citizens' race (the cross-country equivalent of a fun-run), most of them would be badly humiliated by grandmothers and small children. Why? Although runners have the aerobic capacity for cross country, they don't have nearly enough upper body strength needed for poling long distances. Cross country has more in common with rowing and bicycling (together) than running in terms of the muscles employed.

Undeniably, slow jogging and shuffling on skis is the most natural way to learn the rhythm of cross-country striding, even if your first efforts produce only the up-down jogging motion rather than the down-and-back kick and extended glide that are the graceful symbols of this sport.

At first, this sliding and gliding will seem awkward with long boards attached to the feet. I would advise first-time skiers to pick a flat meadow or good set of ski tracks to follow to minimize balance problems the first time out. Set tracks aid stability and direct the forward movement of your skis so you don't have to worry about them and can concentrate on learning to step resolutely onto each gliding ski.

Improving rhythm and balance in the stride is largely a matter of springing forcefully off one ski and centering your upper body weight over the gliding ski —just as you would if you stepped onto a sliding skateboard or vaulted a ditch. The next step is to start using your poles to push yourself along rather than to keep your body from tipping over sideways. The diagonal stride is a continuous fluid movement. But to best describe it, let's break it down into three separate components:

1. *The Kick*—a vigorous down-push on one ski that propels the other ski forward. Like pushing a skateboard.

2. *The Glide*—a free ride on the opposite ski (for the foot that rests on the skateboard).

3. *The Pole Push*—a forceful down-and-back push by the arms, shoulders, and back working together that can add 25 percent to forward power. The pole push is made at the end of the glide.

A   B   C

Diagonal Stride: push down vigorously on the midsection of your skis in the *kick* (A) with the torso leaning forward, and knees and ankles flexed. Drive opposite arms and legs down the track in the *glide,* weight over the gliding ski, forward elbow

From Kick to Kick

Time the explosive downthrust of the diagonal stride just as your skis pass each other. At this moment, your body weight should be centered over your toes and, incidentally, over the balance point of the ski. To depress the ski's camber, don't push with your heels because it will be harder to flatten out the ski base for grip. Your ankles and lower leg should be flexed forward as if you were about to make a basketball jump shot.

More than any other factor, *a good kick results from a forward-leaning torso.* For maximum downthrust, bend your upper body forward to about 45 degrees. It may look like the better skiers are pushing their skis backwards in the kick, but don't be deceived. It's only because they are propelling their bodies down the track so quickly that they leave the trailing leg and ski far behind. Push *down* with the toes and the ball of the foot in the kick; the lower leg will slide back naturally in the glide. You don't need to push it away. Here are some other common mistakes to avoid in the kick phase of the stride:

Lower leg vertical. How can you spring from locked knees?
Weight back on skis. It's difficult to push down effectively on a ski when you're standing up straight—or leaning back—instead of keeping body weight centered over the kicking ski.
The mule kick. Too much back-push, not enough downthrust results in a partial depression of your ski's camber.

The Glide

The purpose of the kick is to launch yourself down the track in a graceful long-distance glide, the stuff that cross-country ski magazine covers are made

slightly bent for a powerful down-compression *pole push* that comes from the shoulders, arms, and upper back. The skier is ready for another kick. The gliding ski becomes the kicking ski (C) and so begins another stride cycle (D, E, F).

of. During the glide, the upper body remains stationary for a moment as it sails over the gliding ski. Your body weight should be centered just behind the ball of the foot.

Experienced skiers talk about keeping their hips "up and forward" during the glide, as if they were being pulled down the track by an invisible rope fastened to their belt buckles. Another way to think about getting your weight over the gliding ski is to concentrate on keeping your butt muscles tight and pressed forward.

What about the trailing ski? We've all seen pictures of skiers with the tail of the rear ski lifted so high in the air—a common error dubbed "bicycling" —that the skier appears poised for a belly flop onto the track. Although fast skiers seem to trail the rear ski back a farther distance than less skilled skiers, actually lifting the rear ski more than a foot into the air means you're over-reaching with your poles or leaning too far forward.

The Pole Push

The glide culminates in a pole plant and backward push that should maintain momentum and propel you forward for the next kick. Watch a good skier as he strides directly toward you. Notice that he plants his poles just to the side of the ski track and that the top of the pole shaft is angled slightly into his body, and not out to the sides.

Watch this skier as he moves by you. He'll plant the pole with a slightly bent elbow. The pole enters the snow in front of the gliding foot in a nearly upright position.

Poling power comes from a unified down-compression of the arms, shoulders, and back. It is not a wimpy backward tug on the pole grips, but a powerful

Relax your grip on the pole handles in striding and double poling follow-throughs. Don't flick your wrists or hammerlock the poles.

The Pole Push: not a pallid back pull, but a forceful uncoiling of the upper body on the pole handle.

down and back driving motion. The motion of the upper body is not unlike the downward-dipping action of an oil derrick. Better skiers pull down on the pole handles and push the grips past their hips with great power. To get in the practice of bringing the muscles of the arms, shoulders, and upper back into play, imagine swinging a hatchet. For power, keep your elbows in close to your body. Relax your grip on the pole handle as it slides by your hip. Swing your other arm forward in an arc for the next pole plant.

For some reason, poling is the most difficult part of the diagonal stride to master. Here are a few of the problems leading to pallid poling:

Roundhousing. Bringing the poles across the chest before the pole plant instead of directing all pole motion straight down the track.

Using poles as props. To support rather than to propel.

Straight-arming. Would you pull a sticky cupboard door open with a straight arm or slightly bent elbow?

Throwing the poles. Flicking your wrists at the end of the pole push is an unnecessary affectation that delays the forward arm swing.

Hammerlocking. This problem afflicts former alpine skiers unused to releasing their grips on the pole handles in the follow-through. Tighten your pole straps so the wrist is snug against the grips.

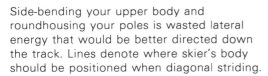

Four Common Errors
When Diagonal Striding

Don't bicycle the kick leg when striding or kick-double poling. Allow the rear leg to relax and straighten at the end of each kick.

Side-bending your upper body and roundhousing your poles is wasted lateral energy that would be better directed down the track. Lines denote where skier's body should be positioned when diagonal striding.

Runner's arm, or having your elbow too bent in the pole push, makes poling weak and ineffective.

Use poles to propel yourself forward, not as props.

Runner's arm. Excessively bent elbows in poling lead to short pole plants and weak back pushes.

Side-bending. Wiggling your upper body from side to side each time you plant your poles. Energy better expended down the track.

Camel-stepping. Skiing with the same-side arms and legs forward—and back.

With practice on snow, the kick, glide, and pole push will soon come together in a glorious moment of truth that tells you you've put the various elements together correctly. The stride is a scissorlike motion that demands an alternating weight transfer from the kicking to the gliding ski. Learn this and you'll move quickly from shuffler to speedster.

The other key move is to keep your weight well forward on your skis, not only as you kick, but as you reach down the track to make a pole plant in front of the opposite, supporting—now gliding—foot. At first, it may help to exaggerate your body's forward lean to force you into the habit of getting out "over the lead ski." In the pole plant, punch the pole tip forcefully into the snow with a slightly flexed elbow. As you drive the pole back, your legs will again slide by one another as you initiate the strong downthrust of the next kick to push the wax or waxless pattern into the snow for grip. This is a new platform from which to spring forward onto the new gliding ski.

Developing Balance and Weight Transfer

Let's retire the old adage "If you can walk, you can cross-country ski." Problem is, too many skiers seem to be following that advice—they're walking, not skiing.

Shuffling on skis is fine for backcountry travel or toting torturous pack loads up mountain slopes. But to add a little pizazz to your skiing, it's time to advance beyond the shuffling stage by developing proper weight shift: the confident weight transfer from the kicking to the gliding ski. To learn weight shift, some skiers need only practice the diagonal stride on a slight uphill section of trail. The hill slows the gliding ski down so it doesn't slide away from the skier, making it easier for him to transfer his weight to it properly—body weight well over the gliding ski.

If this doesn't do the trick, here are some other time-honored methods to develop good balance and weight shift in the stride:

- In a flat track or slight downhill, alternate lifting one ski, then the other, out of the track. Lift the tip of the ski with your boot toe and hold the

Ski without poles to practice weight shift.

ski in the air (about a foot off the snow) for as long as possible. Put the airborne ski back in the track and lift the other ski up to practice balancing on the other foot.

· Try skiing without poles. This is an exercise for skiers of all abilities, especially early in the season when hitting your stride doesn't seem to come easily. Many ski instructors call this exercise "the great ape." The object is to swing your arms slowly and deliberately. Feel your long arms and big mitts pulling you down the track. When you pick up poles again, remember how the lumbering arm swing of the great ape helped to bring body weight forward from the kicking to gliding ski.

Skating: alternately push off the inside edges of your skis, as if your skis were skates, to cover the flats quickly and develop balance.

· Do some skating. Skating is not only an easy way to cover flat surfaces like frozen ponds and meadows, but it demands a dramatic weight transfer from the skating to the gliding ski. When Beth Heiden took up cross-country skiing after the 1980 Winter Olympics, her speed-skating training not only provided her with powerful leg and back muscles for skiing, but the balance to adapt quickly to sliding on longer rails.

DOUBLE POLING

When tracks are fast or lead gently downhill, you can push yourself forward with a simultaneous planting and pushing of both poles. In a race, double poling gives the legs a rest but calls for double duty from the arms and shoulders.

The best body position at the start of the double-poling motion is the same forward-bent trunk as makes single poling in the diagonal stride so powerful. The forward lean allows the skier to rise up on his toes and plant the poles so far in front of the feet that to miss the pole plant would cause the skier to fall flat on his face. The faster you go, the farther in front of your body you'll plant your poles.

The most powerful double-poling motion is characterized by a downward compression on the pole shafts by the muscles of the shoulders, arms, and upper back. The skier appears to fall on his poles, but the result is inevitably a long forward glide on both skis.

Bend your elbows slightly and keep them at this constant angle until you push both poles past your knees. Then straighten your arms as you relax your

Double Poling: use both poles to push yourself forward on flats and slight downhills. The pole plant (A) calls for the same upper body compression as in striding. Unlike striding, you drive both poles past the knees by bending down from the waist (B) in the follow-through (C).

A   B   C

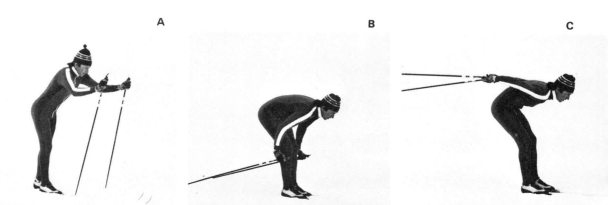

Don't throw the poles away in double poling (A). It wastes time and energy. And don't squat (B). Squatting turns the body into a shock absorber, thereby reducing the power the upper body brings to bear in poling.

grip on the pole handles. Never bend your knees or squat down in the double-poling follow-through. Excessive bending and squatting work like a shock absorber to dampen forward power. It is O.K., though, to flex your knees very slightly to absorb any bumps or rough spots in the trail.

The Kick Double Pole

Use the kick double pole—or the one-step double pole, as it is also called—when the track slows down a bit or you find yourself skiing into a headwind. Many skiers will kick double pole to maintain speed through flat-track corners by scooter-kicking the ski riding the inside track and holding the outside ski in place through the turn.

The double-pole kick should be timed to take place at the same instant you bring the poles forward for the double-pole plant. The timing is not something you need to worry about consciously; it seems to come naturally as you add the kick double pole to your regular double poling on slight uphill sections and

A B

Kick-Double Poling: also called one-step double poling. Add a scooter-kick to double poling on slight uphills and slow snow. Time your kick (A) as you bring both poles forward for the pole plant (B) and driving follow-through (C, D)

to gain speed in slow snow. It's a good idea to practice alternating kicking legs so you don't wear out one leg.

An afternoon of strenuous double poling on an icy track will tell you whether you need more off-season conditioning for the muscles of the arms, shoulders, and upper back. The remedy? More roller skiing, weight training, rowing, or Exergenie (a variable-friction rope device that simulates poling) work when the snow is gone.

STAR TURNS

Here's a beginning turn for the flats that will introduce you to more advanced moving step turns we'll discuss later in the book. The star turn is so named for the pointy, round impression made in the snow after you've completed a 360-degree turn.

With ski tails together, lift one ski tip and place it in the direction you want to go. Bring the other ski alongside. Keep lifting one ski and bring the other ski beside it until you're facing the direction into which you want to ski.

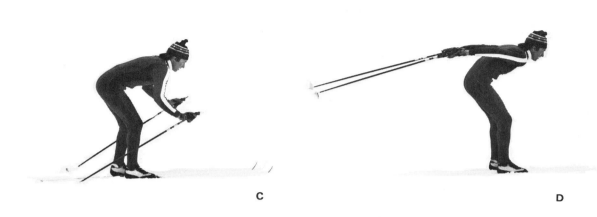

C   D

Star Turns: for stationary turning on the flats, lift up the tip of one ski and place it in the desired direction. Follow with the other.

. . . And Three Extra Tips

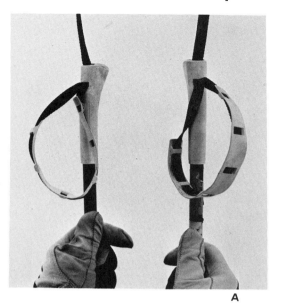 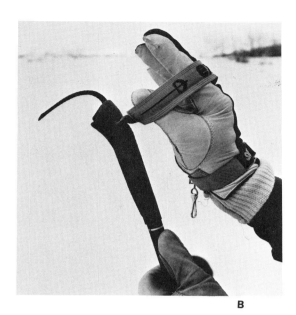

A   B

Pole straps are designed to fit either left or right hands (A). Bring your hand through the bottom of the pole strap to grip poles correctly (B, C, D).

THE PROPER WAY TO HOLD YOUR SKI POLES

This may come as a surprise, but there *are* right and left poles. Look at your pole handles. You'll see that the straps extend from the top of the grip, one on top of the other. How do you know which pole goes in which hand? Simple. The bottom strap goes under your thumb, the top strap rests against the top of your hand. Usually, the top strap will lie over to either the right or the left side to make it easier to tell which pole goes in which hand.

To grip the pole properly, bring your hand up through the pole strap from the bottom and grasp the handle.

Also important: Make sure the pole strap is secured snugly to your wrist so you can release the pole at the end of the poling follow-through and pull it back into your hand without having to hold onto it tightly for fear of throwing it away. Cinch the wrist strap not so tight that it becomes a tourniquet, but just tight enough so the pole grip rests comfortably between forefinger and thumb when you relax your grip.

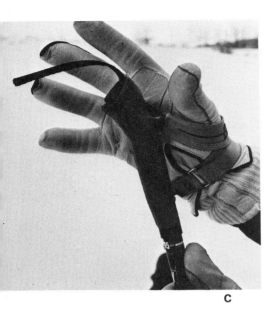

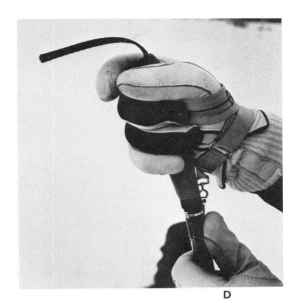

C   D

BEGINNERS, WHY TAKE A LESSON?

Too many cross-country skiers start their skiing careers without proper instruction. The fundamental skills you learn in an introductory lesson will enable you
to ski safely and efficiently and, best of all, with greater enjoyment.

    Novice skiers need advice on how to hold poles properly, how to dress,
and how to fall safely on tricky downhills. After the lesson they can query the
instructor about what trails in the area best suit their skiing abilities.

    Group lessons often begin with an equipment check to make sure everyone
has a right and left ski, a secure boot-binding link, and poles of the right length.
The instructor may also check to see that no one is overdressed and that his
pupils have the right wax for the day's conditions. The lesson may start with
warm-up exercises to limber up tight muscles and familiarize skiers with their
equipment. The instructor may then have you shuffle along the track without
ski poles to practice weight shift. Then it's on to techniques for climbing hills
and safely negotiating your way down them. Practicing ski technique under the
trained eye of an instructor who can point out mistakes before they become
habits is the best way to get off on the right foot in this sport.

HOW TO SKI FASTER

The speed with which you cover the terrain in cross-country skiing depends on the length of your stride, or the actual distance you cover in one cycle of movement from kick to kick or glide to glide, and the tempo at which you ski. Tempo refers to the speed at which you move your arms back and forth.

SPEED = STRIDE LENGTH × STRIDE RATE

From the biomechanical studies conducted under the auspices of the U.S. ski team by Dr. Charles Dillman at the 1980 Winter Olympics, we now know that stride length is a much more important factor in skiing speed than stride rate. In other words, although a beginning skier might move his arms and legs as quickly as an expert, the better skier will travel a much farther distance in the same amount of time. The skilled skier gets much more distance out of each kick and glide. Powerful kicks, good forward propulsion in poling, and long glides account for speed in cross country, not the rate at which you do them.

Putting it all together: rhythmic striding and double poling are the cornerstones of cross-country technique —first learned, hardest to perfect.

Uphill Techniques

The way you handle hills depends on the steepness of the slopes you're tackling and the amount of energy you want to expend. You need not be a bloodthirsty racer to have good hill skiing technique. It's mostly a matter of gaining confidence in your skis and in knowing that the wax will hold when you keep your weight right over the bindings.

Aggressive skiers try to carry as much momentum as possible into hills. They use their arms to supply added power when their skis start to slip. But pack-bearing backcountry skiers would rather keep their heart rates at less than rock-and-roll levels. Touring skiers tack back and forth across the steepest hills, herringbone the soft snow on the sides of trails to get grip and, yes, even walk with skis off when the going is tough. After all, the patron saint of gravity-burdened skiers, Sir Isaac Newton, knew why we shouldn't blow all our energy on the uphills.

THE DOWNSHIFT DIAGONAL

Driving in a car, you'd lose a lot of speed—and likely your transmission—if you downshifted

79

For hills, increase your cadence but shorten your stride length.

D

C

Hill Running: press the ski onto the snow with a flat foot (A) to set the wax securely on hills. Then roll your ankle forward as you slide the opposite leg forward, and reach up the hill for a solid pole plant (B). Keep weight right over skis (C) when driving your body up hills (D) to keep from slipping back.

suddenly from fourth to first gear at the onset of a hill. Many skiers have the same approach to hills. They back it down too fast.

To carry your speed as long as possible and keep momentum going into a hill, hit the intermediate gears as the hill becomes steeper. Shift into lower gears gradually as you shorten the extended stride you use on the flats from running to jogging to shuffling.

Skiing uphill is all kick and no glide. Although your stride rate may stay the same on hills, the amount of distance covered in the glide will be minimal. It's crucial when striding or lightly jogging up hills to push *down* on the snow with a flat foot to set the wax for a moment. If skis start to slip, punch the lead ski into the snow aggressively to flatten the camber more completely. Roll forward over the ball of the foot as you push down on the ski. At the same time you naturally push the opposite, gliding ski up the hill.

Keep the knees and ankles bent and your hips up and forward as you roll forward onto the gliding ski. As you start the next kick, feel the snow surface underneath you with a flat foot. And reach well forward with the poles. If you're using your poles correctly on hills—i.e. keeping them in front of you where they can help most—you should feel as if you're pulling yourself up the hill with a rope. Your shoulders should be slightly rounded, gorilla style, so you can push down and back on the poles with power. This is no time for a wimpy, bent-elbow, "runner's arm" pole push.

B

A

Pitfalls to Avoid in Hill Running

Expert skiers run or trot up hills almost as if they didn't have slippery sticks attached to their feet. But those of us who don't have Olympic racer lung capacity or leg power may look for less anaerobic hill-running techniques. One method that works is to imagine yourself as an Indian scout creeping up on the enemy. The object is to ski with a low profile.

When you come to a hill, slow the pace of the diagonal stride you use on the flats to a half-speed, flat-footed shuffle. Don't bounce up and down as you move forward (you'll be spotted!), but move slowly and steadily upward. Feel your foot press flat against the snow directly underneath you. Then roll forward onto the ball of the foot and spring off it as you reach forward with your pole. Slide your opposite ski forward with a flat foot. Above all, move with the terrain. Sneak up the hill smoothly, quickly, and be light on your skis.

Hills can be tough when the snow is icy or your wax is wearing thin. Assuming that your skis are not too stiff and you're sporting the correct wax, here are a few mistakes to avoid to make hill skiing easier:

1. *Don't bend over too far at the waist.* Keep your weight centered over your skis so you can push the camber down for grip. If you bend over at the waist too far, your weight will be shifted toward the tips of your skis, and if you continue this practice, you'll start slipping backward and fall on your face.

2. *Don't ski too upright.* Stand up straight with locked knees and you'll have a devil of a time applying enough pressure to your skis to make them stick. To propel yourself forward with power, bend your knees and ankles on hills.

3. *Don't look down at your ski tips.* Keep your head up and look at the trail ahead when climbing hills. With your head down, your body will be in the same bent-at-the-waist position that makes it difficult to make skis grip because body weight .is centered over the tips, not the midsection of the skis.

HERRINGBONE AND SIDESTEP

The following techniques are for hills too steep for the downshift diagonal. To herringbone, turn your ski tips outward so they form a V. Your skis will look like they are in a reverse snowplow. Your task is to walk up the hill duck-footed. Your tracks will leave a fish skeleton impression in the snow.

The herringbone reduces the climbing angle of your skis on the snow so the wax has a fighting chance of holding you. Push your poles into the snow behind you for support and added power, and push off the inside edge of each ski as you chop duck steps up the hill. As in the diagonal stride, push back on the pole opposite the ski that is momentarily weighted (and pushed into the snow). Remember to keep your head up and your back straight, and push your ski tips wider apart the steeper the hill becomes. Don't lean forward, as this causes you to backslide.

Herringbone hills that are too steep to walk up (left) and use the running herringbone (a light, duck-footed jog on skis) to climb hills at speed.

The Running Herringbone

In fast skiing, especially racing, the running herringbone is a natural progression from the running uphill stride. You'll also use it often when your skis are losing wax or you just want to blast over the top of a hill.

Each time you spring forward in a running herringbone, you need to make a quick down-compression on the inside edges of each ski to set the wax. You'll find that you really need your poles to provide that extra "oomph" to reach the top of long hills.

On track-set hills, the snow is usually softer at the side of the trail so your skis will hold better. Away from track ruts the snow may also be flatter, giving the skis a greater surface area for wax-snow contact. Short of pulling yourself up hills by grabbing trailside foliage, anything goes when climbing hills. Did somebody say rope tow?

The Sidestep Traverse

On short, steep slopes, and especially in deep snow, you're helpless without the sidestep. This maneuver demands that you stand sideways to the slope you want to climb. With the boot toe, lift your uphill ski and drop it a foot or so up the hill. Use your ski poles to steady yourself. Bring the downhill ski up the hill parallel with the uphill ski. The uphill edge of each ski will cut into the slope and prevent you from sliding sideways. Continue this sidehill stepping until you reach flatter ground.

The sidestep (left) brings even the steepest hills down to size. Chop steps with your ski edges as if you were climbing stairs sideways. Traversing (center) saves energy by reducing the slope angle you must climb. Tacking (right) allows rapid ascents—your skis stay flatter on the snow than in herringboning.

When the hill is very steep or the snow is hard, don't make the common mistake of leaning into the hill with your upper body. Beginning mountain climbers make the same mistake, thinking that by hugging the rock closely they won't fall. They've got it wrong. Skiers and climbers need to keep themselves balanced right over their feet. When sidestepping steep hills, the proper body position makes it feel like you're holding yourself away from the hill.

On longer slopes, combine the sidestep with a traverse. This maneuver is also called the forward sidestep. As you climb diagonally up a hill, step up and forward with the uphill ski. This is an excellent way to gain elevation quickly without expending too much energy.

TRAVERSING AND TACKING

If you walk straight up a hill until your skis start to slip, then turn in one direction or the other until they don't—actually cutting diagonally up the slope —congratulations, you're traversing. Traversing is another method of reducing slope angle so ski wax will hold. There are two traversing strategies. One mode is to attack; the other is to hold back.

Backcountry skiers normally opt for the latter. They'll make long traverses with infrequent switchbacks. Track skiers and racers will often zigzag back and forth up a narrow trail in lieu of herringboning and to take advantage of the soft snow on the side of the trail so their skis can grip. This is the aggressive, time-saving approach to steep hills.

The preferred method of changing direction at the end of a traverse or quick tack is to use a herringbone step turn. Step the uphill ski quickly in the new direction, weight it, then bring the other ski alongside.

The Kick Turn

Learn the kick turn to change direction at the end of a traverse on steep slopes. This can be a tricky maneuver, so practice it on level ground before heading for the hills.

With skis horizontal to the slope, kick the downhill ski forward, lift it into the air, and pivot it so it faces in the opposite direction to your other ski. Brace yourself with your poles; on a hill, you normally hold the poles on the uphill side of both skis to keep them out of the way. The turn is half finished, but this is no time for dallying. Fall now and your friends will have to consult a yoga handbook to untangle you.

Use the kick turn to change direction at the end of steep traverses, or as here, to make a 180 on flat ground.

Shift your weight to the ski you just turned 180 degrees, then quickly swing the other ski around your lower leg until it lines up alongside the other. Phew!

When changing directions at the end of a traverse on steep slopes, you frequently have a choice to make: Should you lift and turn the uphill or downhill ski first? I'd recommend turning the downhill ski first on steep slopes, the uphill ski first on easier slopes. Either way, make sure your skis are perpendicular to the fall line (the route a rolling snowball would take down the hill) before you make the turn so they don't start sliding before you've finished changing direction.

At this European race, one little hill brings out every technique in the book.

5

Downhill Techniques

Down he flies "in Telemark position; one leg forward bent, the other trailing; his sticks hanging like some insect's thin legs, kicking up puffs of smoke. . . ." That's Hemingway, in "Cross Country Snow," describing a maneuver that nearly fifty years later would become a cross-country skiing sensation. But today's cross-country skier may also perform snowplow, stem—even jump parallel turns—on light skis and boots. Recently, cross-country skiers have taken free-heel nordic equipment and downhill turning techniques from the rolling hillsides of North America to make thrilling descents of high peaks in Chile, Nepal, New Zealand, and Mexico. In the U.S., cross-country skiers have counted coup on such venerable giants as Wyoming's Grand Teton and Washington's Mt. Rainier. Will there ever be an end to this derring-do? I doubt it.

For most of us, however, our goal in learning to control these wobbly, skinny staves is not so much to pound moguls at an alpine ski area or run the headwall at Mt. Washington's Tuckerman Ravine, but become as comfortable skiing downhill on trails as we are on the flats and uphills. Most authors who write about cross-country downhilling either advocate difficult-to-master parallel or

87

Deep-powder Telemarking: a once-forgotten cross-country thrill that more and more skiers are rediscovering.

Telemark technique for steep backcountry slopes, or, if the emphasis is on racing technique, assume that you'd be comfortable letting your skis run at 40 miles per hour though a tree-lined chute.

Not I. My premise is that you need a whole bagful of downhill ski tricks to confidently handle a variety of slopes and ski conditions. In this chapter, we'll progress from the simplest foundation moves to more difficult downhill techniques that may take a couple of seasons to master.

BASIC BODY POSITION

Fundamental to being stable on your skis in downhills is a slightly crouched, bent-kneed running position. Keeping your knees bent and flexible, so that your body can absorb sudden terrain changes that would otherwise throw you off balance, is vital to every downhill turn we'll discuss in this chapter. Bent knees make it easier for you to stay over the top of your skis and compress your lower body (and ski camber) into the snow during turns. In later sections, we'll discuss why exaggerated body movements make turning on cross-country skis easier. For now, let's focus on stability.

Let your skis run straight down a gentle hill. Your skis should be spaced six to eight inches apart and your hands held low and out in front of your body. You should feel like you're pushing the back of a chair down the hill. Practice straight running—or schussing, as it is also called—until you can do it without falling.

Stay stable on your skis in gentle downhills with this bent-knee running position.

A   B

The Snowplow (A): keep ski tips together and thrust out your heels to slow down.
The Snowplow Turn (B): drop your hand down by your downhill knee to add weight
(and torque) to the wedge turn.

THE SNOWPLOW

Here is the cornerstone of downhill control. To cross-country skiers, the snowplow is as important as the forehand in tennis, the line drive in baseball, and
the lay-up in basketball. Once you learn to snowplow, you'll be king of steep
hills and corners.

    At first, practice snowplowing on gentle hills with long, flat runouts. From
the straight running position just described, spread the tails of your skis apart
by pushing out with your heels. The skis will form a V-shaped wedge. Keep the
ski tips relatively close together but not touching. To get more plowing power
to slow down, roll your ankles in to set the skis on their inside edges.

    The wider you spread the wedge by pushing out the tails of the skis and
exerting inward ankle power on the ski edges, the slower you'll go. Apply strong
equal pressure to both skis and you'll stop. As in the basic body position, keep
your hips centered between the skis and your upper body erect. Your knees
should be very bent, your hands low and holding the poles out in front of you.

Snowplow Turns

If you apply a little more pressure to one of your skis and actually stand on
it, you will feel it start pointing in a direction other than straight down the hill.
Weighting one ski will make it head away from the fall line (the direct line a
rolling snowball takes down a hill). This makes the snowplow into a turn.

To make the snowplow turn easier, drop the outside hand—i.e., the hand on the side of the ski that is weighted more heavily—down by your knee and apply heel pressure on the same-side ski. Think of the hand on the side of the weighted ski as leading you through the turn. As you swing through the turn in bent-kneed snowplow position, the hand leading the turn becomes the down-hill-side hand.

Experiment with tipping the downhill ski on edge so it will dig into the snow for better braking. Practice turning in both directions. As soon as you complete a turn in one direction, step down on the uphill ski and drop your hand by the same-side knee. Lean to the outside of the turn. To turn more sharply, apply outward heel pressure and roll your ankle in—as if you were severely pigeon-toed—so the ski edges dig in to plow snow away.

The Pole Drag

Skiers in the 1800s were adept at braking with a single long pole. Chances are they used the pole drag on the same kind of narrow, rutted trails for which modern skiers find this maneuver so useful. Many years ago, before the advent of today's lightweight but brittle ski poles, the pole drag was called the "witch's broom" for the pole-between-the-legs Broom Hilda-like stance no longer endorsed by ski instructors because of the potentially crippling effects that a broken ski pole could have on your reproductive capacities!

So take heed, and take hold of your ski poles beside your body, not between

Pole Drag: hold your poles at your sides, not between the legs, to slow down.

the legs, to slow down on hills. With straps off wrists, drag the pole baskets in 91
the snow to slow down. This maneuver adds tremendous braking power to the
basic body position.

Another pole brake technique that works at slow speeds, or when you want
to ease your way down a particularly disturbing section of trail, is the pole
check. From the snowplow position, jab your pole tips into the snow beside the
ski tips. It's almost like double poling in reverse.

STEP TURNS

The pure step turn is nothing more than a moving star turn: sliding down a
hill, you'll pick up the tip of one ski, step it in the direction you want to ski,
put it down and weight it, then pick up the other ski and bring it alongside.
Except in backcountry skiing or lugging a pack downhill (dodging trees, changing direction at the end of a traverse), rarely will you ever use a simple step
turn without adding a skate-push or double pole.

Even at touring centers that set tracks, the tracks in steeper corners will
be washed out, or, as is usually the case, for safety reasons there will be no
tracks at all.

This is the place to use the step turn, especially when you're carrying a
good head of speed into the corner. Make numerous little steps rather than one
or two giant steps to keep from blowing out of the turn. *Keep your feet moving!*
It may help to squat down as you step, but don't sit back on the tails of your
skis—they'll jet out from underneath you. To my knowledge, there are no
awards given for the "goose-step feet-first fall."

On long-radius, slow-speed corners the twin groove tracks may be intact.
But after a number of skiers have rounded the same corner, the track sidewalls
will begin to disintegrate and eventually disappear. On the outside of a downhill
corner, you'll often find grooves diagonaling off the track that mark the spot
where other skiers have pushed off with their outside ski, then transferred to
the inside ski to keep themselves on the trail. This is nitpicking, but an aggressive push-off added to a double-poling motion makes the turn into something
called a *skate turn*. Just trying to hang on and keep the skis in the tracks
without pushing yourself faster? You've made a step turn.

Here's one more use of the versatile step turn—this time to slow down.
At the end of a long sidehill traverse, stop or slow down by stepping your skis
up the hill. Now you can kick turn and head in the other direction down the
hill. Link a few kick turn traverses and you're on your way to making a series

The Skate Turn

A

B

C

D

The skate turn is for survival *and* speed in downhill corners. Add a double-pole push and skate motion as you step the inside ski (A, B) in the desired direction. Bring skis together in the tracks (C, D).

of figure Z's, known as "zorros" to insiders. No cause for embarrassment. Even veteran backcountry skiers use this technique when the snow is too crusty to turn in, or when they're carrying heavy packs.

SIDESLIPPING

There may be no alternative but to skid your skis sideways down the hill on short, steep, or icy slopes. It's not the most graceful way to negotiate a hill, but at least it's solid. Sideslipping is also a prelude to learning proper edge control for parallel turns.

Stand with your skis sideways to the hill. Set your ski edges into the hill by rolling your knees and ankles into the hill. The edges will bite into the snow. Just as with sidestepping uphill, it is important that you lean out over your skis, not into the hill, to keep your weight over the top of your skis. Alpine skiers refer to this sideways bending at the hips while setting ski edges into the hill as *angulation*.

To let your skis slide sideways down the slope, relax your ankles a bit so the edges release their grip on the snow. Your skis will slide more quickly if you relax your ankles more completely because the ski will sit flatter on the snow. You can control how quickly you slide by turning your ankles back into the hill for more edge bite.

STEM TURNS

We've laid the foundation, now let's move on and finish the house. With the snowplow, step turn, traverse, and sideslip, you can safely handle just about every skiing situation you'd encounter on a long tour. Even world-class ski racers resort to the snowplow on scary downhills to keep from launching themselves into trailside snowdrifts; and step and skate turns are the turn of choice for the racing set in rocket-speed corners.

Now that the basic turns have firmly ensconced themselves in your muscle memory, let's add a few advanced turns that combine aspects of most of the turns already described. The *stem turn* looks like a snowplow turn followed by a skis-together traverse—with subtle but important differences. The stem turn is a much more aggressive maneuver than the snowplow. By adding a momentary edge-set (as in sideslipping) to the end of the turn, you give your knees and thighs a "platform" from which to initiate the next turn. You can also utilize angulation on steeper terrain.

A

B

Stem Turn Sequence

C

Stem Turn Sequence: the turn begins with a
skis-together traverse and a downhill pole plant (A, B) to
initiate the turn. Apply weight and stem the uphill ski (C)
so it carves an arc through the fall line (D, E) and
becomes the new downhill ski (F).

D

E

F

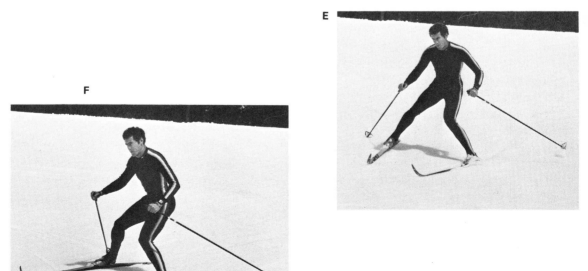

Here's another technique that distinguishes the stem turn from the snow-plow: *anticipation*. That is, facing in the direction of turn—before you actually do it—with your arms and upper body.

Begin a stem turn by traversing across a slope with your weight mostly on the downhill ski and your upper body facing down the hill. Reach forward and down the hill with your downhill ski pole and push the tail of the uphill ski to form a half-snowplow. Weight the ski you've stepped (or stemmed) uphill aggressively.

The stemmed ski now points more directly downhill. Lean out over this ski the same way you did in the snowplow turn. Exaggerate the bending of your knees and press your ankles forward against the boot laces. As your skis swing through the turning arc in the snowplow turn position, your uphill, stemmed ski will become the new outside, downhill ski. Bring the inside ski in parallel to the downhill ski quickly so that the turn is finished with skis together. Now that you're traversing again with your upper body anticipating the next turn by facing down the hill, you're ready to stem that uphill ski again.

The stem turn works beautifully on packed and icy snow. It's not much of a deep snow turn because when you weight your outside ski in the turn, the ski tends to dive. As you grow more confident about your ability to make stem turns, you can move gradually toward *parallel turns* by reducing the width of the snowplow in the turn and by bringing the inside ski close to the outside ski more quickly.

THE PARALLEL TURN

Yes, it's possible to make beautiful, linked parallel turns on skinny skis and low, jogging-shoe-style boots that lift freely at the heel. The key is to realize that stable turns are made by the legs and upper body, and not generated from the ankles.

Skiers with a background in alpine skiing may find it difficult to make parallel turns on thin cross-country skis if they cling to alpine habits like sliding the skis around, banking through turns, or leaning back and turning with the ski tails. High, stiff alpine boots and wide alpine skis let them get away with this technique, but not so cross-country gear. Forget most of the habits of alpine skiing, but remember those that will carry over nicely to paralleling on cross-country skis. The principles I'm referring to are exaggerated knee bending (with little sideways torque on the boots), a powerful commitment to going down and across the fall line, and an emphatic unweighting motion to release the pressure of the skis on the snow at the moment the skis change direction.

Parallel turns grow naturally out of the stem turn. You just use less and less stemming at the start of the turn. You should also add more angulation —or edge-setting and driving of *both* knees and ankles into the hill—at the end of the turn. Some skiers call this move a "pre-turn." This momentary sideslip, ankle-knee rotation into the hill sets up a platform from which you can practically leap into the next turn. Anticipating the turn with your upper body will also help. First I'll describe how the turn works in different snow conditions, then discuss a couple of methods that will make it easier for you to learn how to do it.

On Packed Snow

Parallel turns are easier when the snow is packed because there is less resistance to keep you from swiveling your skis. With today's high, stiff 75-millimeter Telemark boots and metal-edged nordic-alpine (a.k.a. "norpine") skis, there is very little difference between alpine and cross-country parallel technique. If anything, cross-country downhillers get away with fewer mistakes!

Anyway, those corn snow days of springtime are the best time to try out parallel turns. Start by traversing diagonally down a hill with most of your weight on the downhill ski. Concentrate on keeping your downhill knee bent, and hold your skis comfortably apart, as much as a shoulder's width, not jammed together tightly. Face your upper body down the fall line and plant your downhill pole *down the hill and in front of you.* (With long cross-country ski poles you have to reach forward considerably to do this.) You're ready to unweight your skis and turn around the pole just planted.

Let your knees sink down, then raise yourself up and forward and point your ski tips down the hill. By extending your body upward you've taken the weight off your skis so you can pivot them. Keep your upper body facing down the hill so that only your legs and feet have to follow; anticipation creates a springlike force in your thighs that will unwind, adding torque to the turn. With hips and torso facing down the hill, drive your knees and ankles back into the hill to slow down, and, not incidentally, set up for the next turn.

In Deep Snow

If you already know how to ski powder on downhill skis, you'll have no problem adapting your technique to cross-country skis joined to stiff boots. The fun of skiing powder snow on cross-country boards is that you can mix in a few Telemarks with parallel turns.

The difference between skiing powder and hardpack is that you must keep your weight distributed more evenly over both skis when skiing soft snow as

A

B

Parallel Turns

Parallel turns start with an emphatic down-the-hill pole plant (A, B), which triggers the unweighting of skis (C) so they can be pivoted across the fall line (D, E).

C

D

E

there is nothing substantial on which to press down or set an edge. In making parallel turns, everything seems to happen in slow motion. There's a timeless, weightless moment between the time you sink down, plant, up-unweight, and your skis finally arc through the turn. Skiers accustomed to hardpack parallels fail miserably when they try to speed up the turn and crank 'em around.

What to do? First, *concentrate on staying right over your skis.* Don't sit back, but don't lean too far forward either. Bend your knees one hell of a lot. *Exaggerate every move you make.*

From a steep traverse down the fall line, sink down in the knees and keep your shoulders and hips facing down the hill even though your knees still point in the direction of the traverse. Plant your inside pole down the hill in front of you, rise up, and lift your outside pole into the air as if you were making a quick-bid signal at an auction. This is called *up-unweighting.*

Now push your boots slightly ahead of you and down the hill. As you drop into the fall line, you'll catch up to the skis you pushed momentarily ahead of you. Slowly press your knees and ankles back into the hill. Resist the urge to weight the new downhill ski as you come around the turn. A weighted ski will take a dive surpassed only by your own head-over-heels burrowing if you don't remember to keep both skis weighted equally.

How far apart should you hold your skis? I've seen skiers cutting up fields of powder into neat figure-8s who kept their skis pressed tightly together like the downhill skiers of the sixties. Other skiers keep their skis a few inches apart because they think it gives a more stable platform considering the minimal flotation of cross-country skis relative to downhill skis. Experiment until you discover what works best for you.

Learning from Making Garlands

No matter how much you read in books about parallel turns, the only way to learn them is to get out and practice. Fan turns, or garlands, are an excellent way to practice every part of the turn except the troublesome through-the-fall-line moment of truth. After a gradual progression of steeper and steeper turns to either direction you'll be ready to swivel the ski tips across the fall line, that giddy weightless moment when everything comes together or falls apart.

Start from a downhill traverse across the fall line and practice easy, uphill, skis-together turns. Make turns to both sides of the hill and try going steeper and steeper, but don't cross the fall line or ski directly down it.

Practice *tipping your knees uphill* so the ski tips pull you around the turn. Try *carving,* or pressing the ski edges into the snow as you drive your knees and ankles uphill. Try the *hockey stop.* Twist both skis at the same time by thrusting your heels out the same way hockey players bring themselves to an abrupt stop. Plant a pole far down the hill in front of you and practice turning around it.

When you've made plenty of turns in both directions, point the skis down the fall line and turn across it. When you can manage turns straight down the hill, you're ready to start linking turns together.

Jump Parallel Turns

Advanced skiers with accomplished parallel technique use an aggressive parallel turn characterized by a leaping turn initiation that works wonderfully on steep slopes and corn snow to get the skis around quickly. Forceful unweighting (with an emphatic downpush) is vital to freeing the skis from the snow surface for a moment so they can be lifted off the snow and swiveled across the fall line.

Begin the jump turn by crouching very low. Plant the downhill pole far out in front of your body, then spring forward down the hill. The forward leap should give you plenty of momentum to force the ski tips through the turn. Crouch down to make another powerful edge set—the platform from which both you and the ski leave the snow surface for a moment and seem to helicopter across the fall line.

THE TELEMARK TURN

When beginners learn they can actually turn their skinny, wobbly boards in the graceful Telemark position, it's somewhat of a revelation. Awe turns to worship when they also discover the turn's versatility and power. Because nordic boots and bindings allow the heel to lift freely off the ski, the Telemark turn is unique to cross-country skiing.

A couple of seasons ago, some friends and I made a high camp in the eastern Sierra's Rock Creek Canyon. We spent a week making tracks in the

Jump parallel turns begin with such a powerful unweighting motion that the skis lift completely off the snow.

bowls surrounding Bear Creek Spire. One afternoon, two of our party climbed this 13,000-foot peak with skis in their packs, then turned around and skied the same route they had climbed. They used jump turns on the 25- to 30-degree slopes and Telemarked down lower where the slope was more gradual and the snow too soft for parallel turns.

The same spring, 1982, a skier named Rick Wyatt skied the Grand Teton from top to bottom on cross-country skis. Wyatt paralleled most of the way, but Telemarked to bring himself to a stop before two incredibly steep couloirs which he was forced to climb down. I mention these two incidents because I believe we've made too much of the Telemark turn. It's a wonderful survival turn for bad snow. It's a turn that skiers with no downhill skiing background can learn quickly and easily by taking basic cross-country maneuvers, such as the stride and snowplow, and combining them in a new way. But the Telemark is not the all-purpose turn we'd like it to be. Skiers will argue this point, but the Telemark has limited usefulness on the steepest slopes and in icy snow.

The Bicycle Analogy

To begin the Telemark, advance one ski into a snowplow well ahead of your body and steer it diagonally across the tip of the trailing ski. Although you steer with the front ski—and may apply more weight to it on packed slopes to bring the ski around quickly—your weight should fall evenly on both skis. The rear ski carves through the snow. The front knee, bent and driven forcefully into the turn, acts as a moving fulcrum.

In Telemarking, the lead ski is like the front wheel of a bicycle; you turn the forward ski slightly in the direction you want to go. On a bike, your body weight is supported by both wheels, and the rear wheel follows virtually the same path as the front wheel. In Telemarking, again, weight both skis. Steer with the front ski, carve with the rear, and imagine both skis working together as one ski to leave a continuous C-shaped pattern in the snow.

It helps many first-time Telemarkers to think of the forward knee leading the turn. On a gentle slope, to get a feeling for how the turn works, sink down and drive one knee and ski forward. This sounds confusing, but the knee of the forward leg should be over the ball of the foot and the knee of the trailing leg directly below your hip. Don't be tentative—drive that knee forward!

Tips for the First Few Turns

Practice Telemarks on gentle slopes at first. For a left turn, sink down into the bent-knee position, drive the right knee, and ski across the path of the left ski.

The tip of your rear ski should be just forward of the lead ski boot. As you sweep through the turn, rise up, scissor your skis so that a new ski slides forward—maintain the basic body position here—then sink down and bank the ski into the turn.

I've deliberately not mentioned the pole plant until now. In your first few wobbly turns, your poles will serve as crutches to be stabbed wildly into the snow to keep you from tipping over. As you become more stable, you'll want to use a pole plant to initiate the turn and propel yourself into the fall line. In deep snow, some skiers plant both poles at the same time as they step the trailing ski forward and drive it into the next turn. Other skiers plant one pole on the inside of the turn and turn around it as in stem and parallel turns. Whichever way you do it, as a cue to initiate the turn, or as a double pole push, *keep your inside arm low and forward through the turn.* This low arm position is a downhill duplication of the diagonal stride: *opposite arm, opposite leg forward* to keep you centered over your skis despite the fact that they are spread far apart. Keeping your inside arm forward also keeps your upper body faced squarely down the hill. As you complete the turn, bring your outside arm forward for the next single or double pole plant.

I can't stress this poling business enough. It's made a tremendous difference in my own skiing. Good Telemarkers look like they're weaving slowly downhill on a ten-speed bicycle: hands forward and low (gripping the handle bars), knees bent and feet spread apart (resting flat on the pedals), upper body hunched forward but relaxed as it banks into turns following the lead ski.

Running Telemark for Terrain Changes

When you come to a dip in the trail, don't just stand up straight and hope for the best. Drop into the Telemark position to absorb the bump. With one ski

The tip of the rear ski rests just in front of the lead ski boot in packed slope Telemarks. The overall position provides great fore–aft stability for dips and bumps in the trail.

The Telemark Turn

A
B
C
D
E
F
G

The Telemark Turn: on packed slopes, steer with the front ski, carve with the rear (A). As in striding, opposite arm and opposite leg are forward (B, C) in the turn. Plant the downhill pole to begin the next turn (D, E, F) and apply slightly more weight to the forward ski to bring it around quickly (G, H, I).

A   **B**   **C**

Weigh both skis more evenly for powder Telemarks. Here, the skier completes one turn (A) and double poles as she changes lead skis (B) before driving her knee forward and banking into the next turn (C, D).

advanced, your two skis now cover a greater surface area over which to distribute your body weight. And bent knees absorb shock. Ski jumpers have long used the Telemark position for its great fore–aft stability and to absorb the shock of their landings.

Learning to Telemark from the Stride

Telemarking down hills is like striding downhill. To get the feeling of Telemarking, stride down an easy hill. Bend your knees as you slide each ski forward Groucho Marx style. Practice steering into turns by pointing the lead ski across the path of the trailing ski. Pacific Northwest Telemarking pundit Steve Barnett, author of the first book on the subject, calls this maneuver the "crooked stride exercise." Practice striding into Telemarks in both directions.

Telemarking from the Snowplow

The snowplow is also a good starting position for Telemarking. Slide your skis into the familiar wedge position, then advance one ski farther forward than the other and apply body weight to it. Now bring the tail of the trailing ski in close to the tail of the lead ski so the skis work together to carve one continuous arc. Watch the tendency to place too much weight on the lead ski. You can get away with this on low-angle packed slopes, but not when it's steep and deep.

D

Telemarking from the Snowplow

To learn Telemarking from the snowplow,
reduce the wedge angle and slide one ski
forward.

Drive the front knee and hold the opposite side arm low and in front of the body for powerful Telemarks.

Step Telemark Turns

As Telemark techniques evolve, we're going to lose some of the turn's classic grace and style as skiers use the turn on steeper slopes and in deep powder. The step Telemark allows skiers to make fast lead changes, to get the forward ski through the fall line quickly, and to slow down.

In the step Telemark, instead of gliding the trailing ski forward in the lead change at the end of a turn, you must unweight the uphill ski and step it forward and down the hill quickly so it is in the desired arc when you weight it. On steep, packed slopes, some skiers "jump" into Telemark turns; they swivel the lead ski through the fall line in the air. The landing and edging of the lead ski is followed immediately—and sometimes simultaneouly—by the landing and weighting of the trailing ski. It's important to bring the trailing ski alongside the lead ski quickly. The feeling is like stepping a ski down the fall line, walking around it, then squeezing the fore and aft skis together by pressing down with the ball of the foot on the trailing ski.

Establishing Rhythm and Power

It's a lot harder to ski down a slope making random turns than it is to crank one turn after another. If you start to fall in the middle of a Telemark turn, you can often save yourself by immediately banking into another. Think of each turn as a prelude to the next.

In deep snow, you can't put as much weight on the lead ski as you do in packed snow because the ski will dive. How much weight should you apply? It depends on the slope angle and snow conditions. Suffice it to say that if you can feel your toes pressing down on the trailing ski as you swing through a turn, the ski won't slide out from underneath you or cross behind the lead ski as easily.

Power in parallel turns comes from angulation, staying low, and thoroughly unweighting the skis. Power in Telemark turns comes from driving the forward knee into the turn. This is no dainty maneuver. Drive the lead ski forward vigorously with your thigh, knee, and calf muscles. And don't neglect the rear ski even though it is behind you and out of sight. You need the carving power of the rear ski combined with the steering power of the lead ski. The two skis should work as a unit. When the two skis are working together properly, it may feel like the rear ski is actually pushing the lead ski down the hill. When the rear ski tip nestles against the instep of the lead foot, the down-pushing just described is a physical reality.

Common Telemarking Errors

We've all seen pictures of Telemarkers with their hands held high in the air like stick-up victims at a Manhattan mugging. This is only one of many common errors in Telemarking. Briefly described below are the classic errors and a few solutions:

The Buzzard Wing. Hold your hands too high and you raise your center of gravity, making you vulnerable to being thrown off balance. Keep your hands low—your inside hand especially, the one opposite the lead ski— and out in front of your body. You'll still be able to soar.

Arched Back. This problem afflicts skiers afraid to commit themselves into turns on steeper slopes. Keep your weight low, your upper body hunched slightly forward to keep weight centered over skis.

The Buzzard Wing: hands too high, back arched, weight back on skis are a few of the errors here.

Over-rotation. Swing through the turn with only your outside arm forward and you'll over-rotate and fall—usually into the hill—at the end of the turn. Bring the outside arm forward only to make the next pole plant.
Trailing Leg Straight. All those skiers still hooked on the snowplow, repeat after me: "Get down on your knees and turn." And bring the trailing ski tail in closer to the tail of the lead ski so the two skis work as one.
Rear Ski Crossing Behind Forward Boot. You've got too much weight on the forward ski. Weight both skis more evenly.
Can't Turn in One Direction. We all have more power and coordination moving in one direction—and with one or the other foot forward. Water skiers and surfers can sympathize with this problem. Force yourself to practice turns in your least favorite direction.

Think of one turn as the beginning of another—the key to linking parallel and Telemark turns.

Tricks for Tracks and Trails

In Finland a few years ago, traveling and skiing with several other Americans, I experienced a culture of fit and hearty cross-country fanatics. Newspaper and television coverage of cross-country ski competition rivals the American media's devotion to football and baseball. To the Finns, "Mr. October" is a bearded, Bunyanesque fellow named Juha Mieto, a world-class nordic racer who inspires the rhythmic chanting, "Jussi, Jussi . . ." from stadiums full of cold-weather fans.

Nordic ski trails lead everywhere in Finland: out the back doors of factories in the southern half of the country, through city parks (most of which are illuminated for the twenty-four-hour darkness that prevails from November to January), and from hut to hut in the glaciated countryside of the far north. Our Finnish ski guides were the masters of the narrow skis, embodying the legendary outdoor savvy of native Lapps. One in particular, a guide named Peteri, was fearless; he took to the long, steep downhills on a track system in Kuusamo near the Arctic Circle like the jumpers on the 90-meter ramp at Lahti—low, straight, and fast. Only once did he fall, taking the kind of Mach 5 head-first dive that Rickey Henderson might have envied for its great speed and duration.

111

Fast tracking over narrow trails and difficult snow demands that you acquire certain specialized skills known collectively as ski savvy.

We Americans on that trip took the hills and corners a little more conservatively, accustomed as we were to American trails with their desperate drops and right-angle turns in thick trees. But following the example of our intrepid Finn guides, we were soon skiing confidently in a variety of snow and trail conditions—from superbly set tracks over terrain very similar to the American Midwest, to rougher off-trail situations. This chapter is an introduction to situational skiing. We'll open the bag of tricks you'll need to handle those times when all is not just idyllic kicking and gliding over gentle hill and dale. The first part of the chapter focuses on track skiing techniques, the second half on off-trail tricks.

THE HALF-SNOWPLOW

Be not ashamed of such preventive measures as the half-snowplow. Most of us can't ski the downhills as fast as national team skiers. The beauty of the half-snowplow is that it lets you put on the brakes when you're skiing narrow trails or corners where tracks have been set—especially when they've become icy.

The Half-Snowplow: slow down in track-set corners by plowing with one ski outside the tracks.

The trick is to keep one ski in the track while plowing with the other to
slow down. Push *out* on the heel to dig in with the inside edge of the plowing
ski to slow down to acceptable speeds.

The half-snowplow also works on traverses. As you slide across a hill with
skis together, step the tail of the downhill ski down the hill and pressure the
ski's inside edge to slow down.

HIGH-SPEED CORNERING

Maybe you'd like to ski the downhills as quickly and confidently as the national
team skiers—without becoming an ornament in a trailside tree. Noted outdoor
photo journalist Bob Woodward stationed himself at the bottom of a steep
downhill corner at the 1980 Lake Placid Winter Olympics and motor-drove
several rolls of film to see how racers from all over the world skied the same
section of the men's 15-kilometer course.

As you might expect, aggressive, hell-bent-for-leather skiing was the order
of the day. But most of the racers came through the turn in very similar fashion:

1. They kept their feet moving, using rapid step turns.
2. They kept their bodies as low as possible.
3. They seemed to follow their hands and knees through the turn.
4. They stayed close to the inside part of the turn to hold a fast line.
5. They leaned to the inside of the turn to overcome sideways centrifugal
forces.

Maintaining momentum on skis is largely a matter of gaining the confidence to let 'em roll. But proper high-speed cornering technique also helps. For
example, in a sharp right-hand turn, you will keep most of your weight on the
left (outside) ski, and move your right (inside) ski in quick steps to the inside
of the turn. In corners featuring set tracks, it helps to slide the outside ski
forward slightly so your weight is distributed over a larger surface area. Too,
this will enable you to absorb any sudden snow or terrain changes better.

Whoa! Too fast, you say? Build up your confidence for downhill corners
more gradually by slowly reducing the amount of snowplowing and half-
snowplowing you do until you make the switch to speed-maintenance turns like
skates and steps. Trapp Family Lodge (Vermont) ski touring director John
Dostal advises his students to make use of the "bobsled effect" in steep corners.
That is, to ride the banks on corners to check speed. As you improve your
banking ability, move toward the middle and inside of turns to ride a faster line.

High Speed Step Turns

High-Speed Step Turns: keep your feet moving and hold your arms low and out in front of the body to negotiate fast corners.

Don't hold back too much. There comes a time when you've just got to go for it. Follow your hands and knees through the turn. Keep your feet moving. And stay low—if you fall, you won't have as far to go.

THE TUCK

Tuck for Speed

Wind tunnel tests conducted periodically by the U.S. ski team show the classic egg tuck to be the most streamlined body position for holding or increasing speed on long downhills. You can also relax and catch your breath when holding a tuck.

Ripping along fast downhills on skinny sticks is . . . well, it's a blast. One moonlit night in the Sierra above Lake Tahoe, a friend and I tried to find the perfect tuck position on a gentle slope that tapered onto a frozen meadow. With our gloves we marked relative distances traveled on the hard snow (as if testing speed waxes for glide before a race). We discovered that we traveled farthest and fastest when crouched low with elbows held just below the knees, poles held horizontal to the snow, and pole grips held together in front of the face so the pole shafts flared back in a V. Admittedly, we also got a lot of speed and distance by squatting down on our skis, but this would be a vulnerable position on a bumpy ski track.

Racers use the low egg tuck. The trick is to keep your head up and eyes pointed down the track. Keep your weight over the middle of the skis, or, when the situation allows—as on a gentle downhill—slightly on the tails of the skis. Tail-weighting seems to give more speed. There's no reason why even a first-time skier shouldn't be able to adopt the egg position easily.

Tuck for Rest

Use the resting tuck to recover after heart-taxing uphills in races and long exercise tours. Skiers call this the "marathon tuck" because they may be too tired to hold the speed tuck position at the end of a long day.

Your rear end is held a little higher off the snow in the resting tuck—a much less aerodynamic position with big-hipped cross-country types! Elbows rest on the knees. And if you're really whipped, you can rest your whole upper body on the knees. Here are a few mistakes to avoid in both the resting and the speed tuck positions:

The low egg position (left) is the most aerodynamic for downhill speed, while the resting tuck (center) gives your body a breather on slight downhills. The reverse shoulder tuck (right) centers body weight over the inside ski in long radius turns.

1. *Don't cross your hands.* Hand-crossing is an outdated, nonaerodynamic skiing style.

2. *Don't stand up too straight.* Keep your knees bent deeply so you won't be thrown off balance by sudden bumps.

3. *Don't drop your hands too low.* This will cause your pole baskets to drag through the air like flags. Your hands will also drag air, slowing you down.

Reverse Shoulder Tuck

Canadian team coach Marty Hall has resurrected an old alpine ski technique that citizen racers and light tourers can use to maintain the speed of the tuck through long-radius high-speed turns where there is a set track. The technique works best in corners that are not very steep.

In a reverse shoulder tuck, your *hands and upper body face toward the outside of the turn,* but *knees and hips point in the direction of the track you're following.* The theory behind this seemingly awkward maneuver? The reverse shoulder helps hold your skis against track sidewalls because your body weight is centered over the inside ski in the turn.

THE MARATHON HALF-SKATE

In March 1981, Bill Koch skied 50 kilometers in just two hours on a flat course near Putney, Vermont. He did it by half-skating the entire distance. Like a kid pushing a scooter, he left one ski in the track and pushed off powerfully with the other.

C

A

B

Banned in Oslo: the marathon skate is so effective the Scandinavians have tried to banish it from international competition. With one ski in the track (A), skate-push the other ski at the same time you double pole (B, C).

The "Koch Skate" is not really a new technique. European long-distance skiers have been using the half-skate for years. When Koch and fellow ski team member Doug Peterson saw the effectiveness of half-skating at European races in the late seventies, they brought the half-skate to the States. But Koch repopularized half-skating worldwide by winning the Engadin Ski Marathon on a flat course in Switzerland, then the World Cup in 1982, largely on his ability to smoke across the flats and gentle uphills. Since then—and perhaps out of spite—the Scandinavian countries have worked to ban marathon skating in international ski competitions and have threatened to rough up the outside of ski tracks to make skating more difficult.

Half-skating is a valuable technique for any distance you may want to ski, not just marathons. The half-skate may as well be called the skate double pole because you push backwards with both poles as you push out to the side with one ski. You can get a tremendous push down the track by skate pushing and pole pushing vigorously (and simultaneously) and throwing your upper body forward over the gliding ski. After the skate push, bring the ski back just outside the track and compress the skating leg over the ski just before kicking sideways and back.

In long races on relatively flat courses, half-skating is faster than striding or double poling.

Half-skating also works in the backcountry far from machine-set tracks. With a heavy pack, I once skied down a long canyon in the eastern Sierra by half-skating a firm, skier-set track. It broke the monotony of striding and double poling a long distance in fast conditions.

CHANGING LANES AND PASSING

Your mission: To search out better tracks and pass slower skiers. But how to overcome the awkward feeling of picking up your skis and pushing them across ruts and snow chunks when you lack the balance of Baryshnikov? The key is to wait until you ski to a place where the snow is smooth between lanes. In other words, find the freeway flats.

Ski aggressively into the new tracks. Don't wobble and hesitate. Try to maintain down-the-track momentum. When you find a good spot, lift the ski on the side of the new tracks and slide it diagonally across *both* new tracks.

Passing

A

To pass or change lanes, ski across both new tracks (A), then put the inside ski back in the track and move along (B, C).

B

C

Make a bold weight shift onto that ski. The forebody of the stepped ski will slide beyond the new tracks, giving you the room to bring the inside ski and place it directly into the track. Now bring the outside ski into the track.

If the tracks are old and rough or you're changing lanes on a downhill stretch, stay in a low body position to absorb any undue undulations. Ski first across both new tracks with the outside ski, then bring the inside ski into the new track without losing momentum. At the intersection of a new trail, time your move into the new track so the placement of the inside ski into the track is a forceful leg drive down the track.

A word about overtaking slower skiers. The days when you could simply bark "track" and the poor, straggling skier would step out of your way are long gone—except in races when this behavior is expected. Yelling "track" is a rude intrusion on a quiet ski trail. It scares people. The next time you come upon a shuffling skier, try clearing your throat or coughing. For me, heavy breathing and wheezing noises seem to work; most skiers give plenty of room to anyone on the verge of collapse.

Bust the lead ski free of deep snow and step it forward gingerly when breaking trail.

BREAKING TRAIL

Now we plunge into the Great Untracked and fill your ski bag with off-trail tricks. Busting trail in deep snow is much more tiring than romantic, even though your destination may be some giant untracked powder bowl in a fairyland of snow-flocked trees and jagged peaks.

Ski with a group of friends so you can change lead skiers frequently. This is *leapfrogging*. After breaking trail until tired, the lead skier steps off the trail and waits until the parade has passed him by, then steps back in line. Having done your bit for the good of the group, it's time to catch your breath.

In very deep snow the leader will have to break his ski tip free of the snow before sliding it forward over the snow surface until he's ready to stand on it. This can be exhausting. If the snow is wet and deep, don't ski alone and don't try to ski very far. Remember that if you get tired, you can always ski home the way you came in—on the tracks you just packed.

SKIING THE TREES

Can you imagine catching a pole basket on the door handle of a passing car? That's what it feels like to snag a pole on a bush as you ski by. Take the straps off your wrists before skiing wooded trails or thick pine groves so you don't dislocate a shoulder. The trick of keeping your thumb outside the pole straps is also safe. You can still slip your hand free if you catch a pole basket.

Steer clear of tree wells, those giant depressions that form around the bases of trees when the snow is deep. And wear glasses or goggles to protect your eyes from getting scratched by vegetation.

HANDLING ROUGH TERRAIN AND BAD SNOW

The seasoned cross-country skier knows how to make the best of what he's got, even if that means less than perfect snow, steep trails, ruts, and bumps. Mastering everything that is difficult in the winter world will give you a great feeling of accomplishment and round out your skiing skills as well. Besides, if you ski only on weekends a couple of times a season, you may more often than not hit ski days with marginal conditions. So make the best of them.

Difficult Snow

Adapting your technique to ice, crud, "mashed potatoes," "Sierra cement," and bottomless-depth hoar (the most notorious rotten snow imaginable, created when the warm spring sun forms a crust over deep, porous snow) takes time and patience. I've raced in citizen races on courses that were so icy that to slide off the trail at any turn threatened serious joy-riding through the trees, not to mention certain bodily injury. No wax available was capable of providing purchase; double poling and skating (this is telling!) were the only means of forward propulsion. I've heard nightmarish tales of skiers making 200-mile backpack trips across the Yellowstone Plateau on which their skis broke through a thick crust and plunged two feet with every step.

I skied the icy race course with the same care that you would pilot a car home in a snow storm: no sudden moves, no bursts of speed. Those Yellowstone skiers had to break camp before dawn every day and ski as far as they could (keeping to the trees that had shaded the snow a bit) by stepping on the snow as if crossing thin ice on a pond.

Be versatile in difficult snow conditions. Read the snow and match your technique to it. On ice, expect your skis to slide. Don't try to dig your ski edges in until you reach a patch of snow where they will hold. Ski from snow patch to snow patch. In crusty or wet snow, forget making pretty linked turns. Get your boards around by lifting (stepping) them, or jumping and Telemarking as best you can.

In fast-changing snow conditions, your skis will often ice up underfoot. One method to rub the snow clump from the ski base is to ski over a companion's skis—if he or she will let you. Otherwise you can scrape your own skis together without taking them off by crossing them over one another in pigeon-toed fashion.

Sit down to fall: head-first falls are no picnic. To fall safely, land on the ample padding of your buttocks (A, B) to the sides of your skis. Keep your poles at your sides (C).

C

Good skiers are like gravity warriors; they know that dips and sudden flat runouts from steep slopes are full of insidious downward G-forces that will try to pitch them forward. Battle the forces of gravity when skiing from steep to flat by sitting back slightly and absorbing the downward compression with your knees. Use the same technique when skiing off a packed trail at high speed into slower deeper snow.

Savvy skiers also take notice of seasonal and thermal effects on snow conditions. Tree drip, for example, causes slick spots under trees during springtime. Snow that is warmed by the sun is slower. Before skiing into a slow spot, try to stay low and back on your skis a bit. Anticipate the sudden acceleration of skiing into faster, shaded snow by rocking forward onto the skis and bending the knees.

THE CONTROLLED FALL

Falling is O.K. We all do it. In fact, it's one of cross-country skiing's most preferred stopping methods. An excellent faller is as much respected among his peers as the daredevil chute-shooter or ten-time Birkiebeiner veteran. Question is: How to fall safely?

A

B

To get up from a spill, get your skis below you on the hill, across the fall line. Make an X with your poles in deep snow to push against (A, B), then rock back on your heels (C) to stand up (D).

A

B

C

Getting Up from a Fall

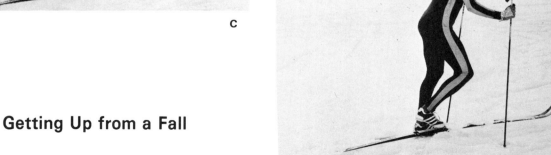

D

Clearly we're not advocating the head-first Rickey Henderson dives of Finnish ski guides or the truly out-of-control. Head-first toboggan runs on your front zipper are a good way to injure wrists and thumbs—as well as other vital body parts! And those pointy little ski tips? They are right at eye level in one of those nasty nose dives. Better to sit back on your tailbone and actually *lower* your body to the snow as if you needed a little more time to sit down and plan strategy for that tricky downhill ahead.

When you touch down, roll over on your side and keep your arms and poles out of the way. Relax and ride it out.

Getting up from a fall, especially in deep snow, can be a little tricky. Skiing with a heavy pack? Take it off before trying to get up. If your head ends up down the hill, swing your skis in the air and get them below you, side by side. In deep snow, make an X with your poles on the uphill side of your skis just in front of your body. The X gives you a little platform to push on. Crawl out over the front of your skis with your weight centered over your knees. Rock back on your heels to stand up. Use your poles for balance and to pull yourself up.

Fence Vaulting

Fences are a common obstacle once you leave the comfort of prepared tracks. In negotiating them, you may opt for the more cautious one-ski-at-a-time approach.

7

Conditioning for Cross-Country Skiing

When evening came it was time for training. In heavy working boots and overalls it was right off through the forest, up the mountainsides and then back to the forest cabin which I lived in when I was out on forest work. . . . When the sun came up it was time to begin chopping wood again. And when evening came a new training session was waiting. . . . Sometimes I stuffed as much food as I could into myself in the morning and took off on a long tour of four to five hours; sometimes the devil possessed me, and if I came to a lake which wasn't overly wide, I swam across it instead of running around it.

—Swedish ski hero Sixten Jernberg, as told to Lennart Strand in *Training for Nordic Skiing*, World Publications, 1975

Very few of us have the time or opportunity to train as energetically as Sixten Jernberg. But to motivate yourself to add even a brief ski conditioning program to your daily schedule would require only that you see two pictures of yourself—one at the start of a long race or tour, and one at the finish. No matter how accomplished your technique as track skier or Telemarker, it's all for naught if you're too tired to put it together halfway down the trail.

The purpose of this section is to give you plenty of ideas for an effective exercise program that will require little time investment compared to the benefits accrued—namely, the power and endurance to ski well, and the muscle strength around joints and ligaments to keep you from injury.

129

Summer training wheels: roller skis closely approximate on-snow kicking and gliding.

THE UPPER BODY

Carol Duffy, from Hayward, Wisconsin, the forty-five-year-old mother of eleven children, turned the citizen racing world on its ear by becoming the first person to complete all nine World Loppet ski marathons and finished seven of the nine league races in the winter of 1979. But as Carol remembers, she was

Powerful, not bulky, upper body muscles will help you ski better.

Trapezius

Deltoid

Latissimus Dorsi

Triceps

only "just barely hanging on" at the end of each race. Carol had spent the summer before her first marathon ski season running the wooded trails near her home in northern Wisconsin.

She changed her training before skiing the final two races of the Loppet series in 1980, adding roller skiing, weight lifting, sculling, and running with ski poles to her regimen. The reason? She realized the importance of building muscles more specific to cross-country skiing: the arms, shoulders, back, and abdomen that comprise the upper body.

At the 90-kilometer Konig Ludwig Lauf in West Germany, Duffy felt strong through the entire distance. Two weeks later she skimmed an hour off her previous best time in the 55-kilometer American Birkiebeiner to capture the number one World Loppet medallion. In cross-country skiing, upper body strength spells success.

BASIC TRAINING PRINCIPLES

Training for cross-country skiing need not be as spartan and rigorous as a Marine boot camp. It can be fun. Realize only that cross country is an energy-demanding sport and that your ability to enjoy it will be enhanced if you have a strong enough cardiovascular system to resist fatigue.

Cross country is also a power sport. A good stride is the result of a strong kick, a long glide and a forceful pole push. (For herringboning and skinny ski downhilling you also need strong thighs, calves, hamstrings, and butt muscles.) Therefore, cross-country ski training should build both muscular strength—the strength to perform ski movements—and muscular endurance, the capacity of your muscles to repeat those movements many times.

Sports-medicine authorities have been proclaiming for years that cross country is better than almost any other sport in the way it improves your aerobic capacity—better than running, swimming, or cycling. But unless you spend the summer months skiing on glaciers, or make sojourns every spring to the southern hemisphere, you'll have to use running, jogging, and other forms of dry-land exercise to stay in shape for the next ski season. If you're new to any of the forms of exercise I'm describing, start slowly so your body can adjust to the initial stress and discomfort.

Whether you're bound for the Olympics or an upcountry ski weekend, adhering to the following training principles will make your workouts more effective:

- *Specificity.* Practice skills that duplicate as closely as possible the movements you will perform out on track or trail. The corollary to this principle is that time spent strengthening muscles not vital to technical improvement or injury prevention is wasted. You don't need grapefruit-size Arnold Schwarzenegger muscles to ski cross country. Enlarging the wrong muscles actually pulls oxygen away from muscles necessary for skiing.
- *Regression.* "Use it or lose it." That's why you should roller ski and run with ski poles in the off-season. Train regularly to maintain muscle tone and cardiovascular fitness (the ability of the heart and lungs to deliver oxygen to the muscles).
- *Individuality.* Not everyone responds to the same program in the same way. Just as we are all different in terms of motivation, body structure, and genetic background, so we are different in the kinds of training routines we need to keep in shape.

Six Training Tips

Before you rush out to pump iron, chop wood, or bike fifty miles, consider the following advice from athletes who have made training mistakes and coaches whose job it is to be one or two steps ahead of the athletes.

1. *Don't overtrain.* As Bill Bowerman, the great University of Oregon track coach, advises his runners: "Train, don't strain." Try to hold back a bit and save a little energy for your next training session. Obsessive trainers are the first to burn out, and the first to fall prey to injury. If you regularly monitor your resting pulse rate and it starts to rise rather than fall or hold steady, back off for a while.

2. *Alternate hard and easy days.* Your muscles need time to recover after a day of hard training. Go hard one day, then rest or go easy the next.

3. *It's quality, not quantity, that matters.* Apply this principle to both strength and power training whether it's hill running or weight lifting. Five miles of hard running is worth far more than ten miles of slow jogging.

4. *Overload to ensure gain.* "No pain, no gain." Sounds like the opposite of "train, don't strain" but actually refers to the way your muscles respond to work. To make your muscles stronger and build endurance, increase the intensity of the workout. Force the heart and muscles to adapt to the new workload.

5. *Begin dry-land training in the spring, but increase the specificity and intensity of your workouts in the fall.* Have fun in the spring. Hike, run, swim, and take long bike tours with your friends. Come September—and to make the

transition from asphalt to snow easier—make a shift from longer, less intense workouts to shorter, more intense and specific workouts.

6. *Variety spices your training.* Boredom decreases motivation. Many sports are compatible with skiing. Don't deny yourself the pleasure of enjoying soccer, tennis, canoeing, kayaking, climbing, and backpacking in a single-minded devotion to cross-country skiing.

BEYOND RUNNING

The more oxygen your heart and lungs can supply to the muscles—and the faster they do it—the more fit you are. Running is probably the easiest way to get this cardiovascular advantage. Just slip into a pair of padded running shoes and off you go.

Unfortunately, many of us don't make the most of running. We plod along, barely bringing a sweat to the brow, avoiding steep hills, and never pushing it on the flats. Or worse, we rely *too much* on running to get us in shape for skiing, and neglect the upper body muscles so important in striding and double poling. Very few serious runners make a transition onto skis commensurate with their successes on the roads. Nor are cross-country skiers the fastest runners. Too much upper body is often to blame.

But certain running strategies are very useful as ski training. Since cross country is a series of high-effort periods of striding, herringboning, and climbing followed by downhill rest periods, it's very similar to interval-type running in terms of heart exercise. By intervals I mean repeated hard exercise interspersed with rest or less intense exercise (the kind where the heart rate drops below 120 beats per minute).

Natural Intervals

In training for skiing, try running more hills, summer hiking trails, or naturally rolling terrain. Maintain good pacing on the flats, but really push it on the uphills—right over the top. Coast down the other side as you would in skiing.

Hill running hurts because it forces the muscles to work anaerobically (without oxygen). The resulting lactic acid build-up in the muscles causes a burning sensation. You'll know when you're pushing into this valuable anaerobic work when you can no longer carry on a conversation with a running companion. By improving your ability to push it on tough hills, you'll ready your body for similar exertion in skiing.

Don't live in a hilly area? Run intervals on a track. The idea is to run full speed for a short distance at your maximum heart rate, then jog until you catch your breath. (It should take between thirty and ninety seconds to get your wind back. If your heart continues to beat quickly and doesn't return to 120 in this time, terminate the workout.)

Ski Striding with Poles

Take your ski poles with you the next time you run. It makes running more specific to skiing. Running up hills with poles is mostly anaerobic work, and great exercise for the legs, shoulders, and arms. The preferred technique is to stay low to the ground, simulating the low-profile uphill stride. Land on the heel of each foot as you stride up the hill.

Reach up the hill with your shoulder, arm, and upper back working as a single unit. Compress down and back vigorously on the ski poles to work the tricep, deltoid, and latissimus muscles. You can hold your poles at your sides for quick sprints on the flats.

Hill running with poles is valuable off-season training. To more closely simulate skiing, slow the tempo down to a low-profile stride. Land on each heel and roll forward from the ankles as in ski striding uphill.

Move with the terrain on roller skis. Practice striding on slight uphills and double poling the flats and downhills. Also try skating.

Roller Skiing

Roller skiing duplicates the total movement of cross-country skiing better than any other off-season exercise. After all, it *is* skiing . . . on roads. Not only does roller skiing result in a much better muscle-memory carryover to snow than running, but it is far less bone-jarring as well.

Roller skis are about three feet long—as long as the kick zone on a ski—cost between $125 and $175, and have a ratchet mechanism in the hubs of the front wheel that allows the ski to roll forward but prevents it from sliding backward. Thus roller skis simulate kicking and gliding.

Current roller ski models are made of laminated wood or tubular aluminum and have hard rubber tires about five inches in diameter designed for smooth asphalt surfaces. You can use any boot/binding combination with today's roller skis, but most skiers prefer narrow racing bindings because of the excellent tracking control and the fact that the shoes that fit them are lighter and cooler for warm-weather skiing.

Remove the baskets on your poles for better poling follow-throughs. Poles with carbide steel tips give the best grip on roads, last a long time, and can be resharpened. A couple of manufacturers make special roller ski poles with spring-loaded ferrules. The shock-absorbing feature of the special poles may protect your wrist and elbow joints from excessive jarring. Another recommendation: ski with the pole straps off your wrists in case you jam a pole tip in a manhole cover or crack in the pavement. Otherwise, your shoulders will pay a stiff penalty.

Most roller skis don't have brakes. The one model that does features an upraised bar behind the heel which is activated by pressure from the lower calf and exerts drag on the rear wheels. But you have to lean back considerably to make them work—not my idea of a safe downhill body position. Never fall if you can avoid it. As Art Dickinson, director of Colorado University's Human Performance Lab, once remarked after nursing back to health yet another Boulder road roller: "A fallen roller skier's body looks like it rolled around on a row of bacon slicers, and he usually donates enough hide to the pavement to supply three plastic surgeons with a year's worth of graft material!" I'm not advocating that you ski around town in head-to-toe motorcycle leathers when sweat pants and light gloves will provide a goodly measure of protection in falls. Just practice double poling, skating, and racing tucks on *gentle* downhills.

How to Use Your Training Wheels

Ski as the terrain dictates. Build leg power with the diagonal stride on long gradual uphills. Double pole the flats. As with any endurance activity, you should progress gradually. If you've been running, begin roller skiing half your daily running distance until your back and shoulder muscles get used to the kind of abuse your legs have come to know. But since energy expenditure in road skiing is significantly less than in snow skiing, and if you plan to race this winter, your road mileage should soon approach the length of expected races. A program I've used with success is to alternate days of running or biking with a day of roller skiing to build a balance of cardiovascular fitness and specific muscle strength. As winter approaches, serious trainers will break up the steady-state endurance-building workouts with strength-building interval workouts.

There are as many pitfalls to avoid in roller skiing as in every other cross-country movement—with the following additions:

1. Well-traveled, poorly paved roads.
2. Developing a late "scooter-style" kick because the roller ski ratchet mechanism guarantees good "purchase" without a vigorous down-and-back leg extension.
3. Bad balance and incomplete weight shift. Roller skis wander a bit. Don't worry about it. Concentrate on getting forward over the lead ski and simulating the fully extended kick and the driving follow-through that will give you a decided advantage when you ski on winter's first snow.

Do your arm, stomach, and lower back muscles become sore after the first long tour or race of the season? If so, you need to add strength training to your preseason exercise program. Weight training not only builds muscle power but, more important for skiing, builds muscle endurance which will give you the ability to perform ski movements repeatedly over time.

Where to do it? If you're new to weight training, I'd suggest joining the local health club or YMCA, and working with an instructor who can guide you through a beginning program. Tell him you are a cross-country skier and need to strengthen your upper body.

You can also do weight work at home. Invest the local fitness center's healthy membership fee in a set of free weights instead. Experienced weight lifters prefer free weights because more balance and coordination are needed to keep the barbells stable than with the guided weight machines such as Universal, Nautilus, and Cam II. But if you haven't trained with weights before, at least start with the machines, and progress to free weights as you gain experience.

There are so many different muscle groups used in cross-country skiing that to isolate and describe any one would demand frequent referral to an anatomy handbook. Just think of the muscles you use in striding, double poling, herringboning, and Telemarking. Almost every muscle in your body, right? For poling, it's the muscles of the shoulders and arms, specifically the "lats," "traps," "delts," triceps, and wrist muscles. (If you're not sure which muscles I'm referring to, just refer to the photograph depicting upper-body muscles or try the weight-training moves described below.) In all phases of skiing, the abdomen and lower back muscles support the upper body. And in kicking and gliding you need strong quadriceps, calves, and hamstrings.

Suggested Weight Stations and Routines

The following weight movements are the most effective at strengthening muscles vital for skiing. Try to work out three times a week with a day off between sessions, even if you have time only for sit-ups, push-ups, dips, and backlifts in lieu of a more time-demanding weight-training session.

It's also a good idea to alternate workouts. You might pump heavy weights at eight to twelve repetitions one day, and pound lighter weights for up to thirty repetitions on other days. Vary your routine to build a balance of strength and

Weight and Machine Work for Cross-Country Skiing

The Nautilus double chest machine builds pectorals for poling.

Wrap a rope around the universal pulley chin bar and pull light weights to build the latissimus muscles.

Bent rows: standing position.

Cam II upper back machine.

Dips can be brutal but they build strong triceps.

Lateral dumbbell raise.

Universal leg press.

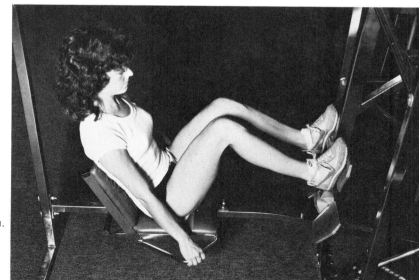

Cam II knee extension.

endurance. Then in late fall just before the snow flies, work on your endurance (almost to the exclusion of the strength workouts) with light weights and frequent repetitions.

Be sure to warm up thoroughly before lifting. Jog or ride your bike to the gym. Do some stretching. You can do most of the following lifts either in the gym or at home. I've indicated the areas of the body that receive benefit and the types of weights needed to perform these moves:

Bench press. Builds pectorals and triceps for poling power (Universal or free weights).

Shoulder press. Builds triceps, deltoids, and trapezius muscles used in poling (Universal, Nautilus military press, or free weights).

Arm dips. One of the best tricep workouts going. Be sure to lower the upper body until your chin is level with bar, then rise up without swinging the legs (Universal dip station or lower yourself between chairs).

Pulley chins/lat pulls. Strengthens latissimus muscles for poling. Wrap towel or rope around bar, pull toward you to simulate poling (Universal).

Rows. Builds trapezius and deltoid muscles in the upper back. Keep hands four to six inches apart (Universal or free weights).

Squats. Exercises almost all leg and butt muscles. Warm up thoroughly by stretching and squatting without weights. Use light weights at first and keep back straight (Cam II or free weights).

Tricep dumbbell swing. Lie stomach-down on bench. Raise dumbbell off floor and swing back toward hips with slightly bent elbow as you would in poling.

Leg press. Start with low weights to avoid knee injury (Universal).

Other exercises. Hamstring curls (Nautilus or Universal), calf-raisers (Universal), ankle extensions (Universal), leg extensions (Universal or Nautilus).

Exercises to Do at Home

If time is limited, or you just can't handle the muscle-bound machismo of the local gym's weight room, you can still train effectively at home with the exercises described below. The first two, sit-ups and backlifts, should be part of your weight training routine at the gym:

Home Exercises for Cross-Country Skiing

Do sit-ups with legs bent or draped over a chair to work different abdominal muscles.

Back raisers, never past horizontal, strengthen lower back muscles.

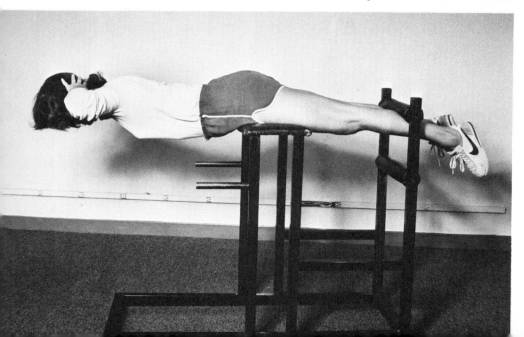

Friction rope devices are
popular for home workouts.

Build your own roller board to strengthen the upper body. Do this exercise on either
your stomach or your knees to build different muscles in the arms and back.

Incline Sit-Ups

Do sit-ups on an incline board with knees bent to isolate the abdominals. Or drape your legs over a chair. With both hands behind your neck or at your sides, pull yourself up with your abdominal muscles, not your thighs.

Back Extensors

Always follow sit-ups with backlifts to strengthen the opposing lower back muscles that support your upper body. Hang your body off the end of a bench or table and pivot at the waist to lift your trunk up to a horizontal position. Don't lift past horizontal; it could strain your back.

Try to do these exercises plus arm dips, pull-ups, and push-ups every other day, especially if you don't have access to a gym. Do them during the ski season during the days and weeks when you can't go skiing.

KEEPING A TRAINING LOG

It's a good idea to keep an objective record of your training. Why?

1. It's the simplest way to monitor your progress.
2. You can avoid overtraining or injury.
3. Based on past experience, you can predict when you're going to feel best for a long race or tour by studying the types and length of the training that lead up to high-performance days and then duplicating that training so the good days happen again.

You can keep a training log in an appointment calendar or make copies of a weekly log sheet of your own devising. Keep tabs on your resting (morning) pulse rate, hours of sleep, lengths of workouts. Include some objective comments. Did you move easily up the hills? Were you drained of all energy? Are you improving? Is work-related or emotional stress affecting your training? Some skiers compile not only weekly and monthly training totals, but yearly totals so they can look back over a long period. Keeping a log is fun. It puts you in touch with your body.

Friction-Resistance Devices

They have a variety of names: Exergenie, Exergym, and Exel Exerciser. These variable friction rope devices have an aluminum cylinder or some other adjustable tension-setting feature that grips the rope to make it harder or easier to pull the rope back and forth to simulate cross-country poling.

I like to set the resistance high enough on these devices so my arms are shaking after two or three minutes of vigorous pulling. You can also set the resistance lower and pull the rope for half an hour—if you don't mind staring at the wall for that long.

Similar in their effect on the arms are the highly revered "Putney arm bands": rubber bicycle inner tubes cut then tied around the limbs of an available elm tree. Arm bands were invented by former U.S. coach John Caldwell and are part of the training routine of many a U.S. ski team member in the Putney, Vermont, area. What's nice about arm bands is that you can pull both bands at the same time to build double-poling power.

The Sauna

Relax. You deserve it. The steamy confines of the sauna are as much a part of cross-country skiing as knickers and reindeer sweaters. Substitute a hot shower, bath, redwood tub, or Jacuzzi if birch flogging and snow rolling isn't your bag.

MONITORING YOUR PULSE RATE

Check your pulse rate to get an immediate reading on how your training is going—in the morning when you wake up and in the middle of tough training sessions.

Most of us have average resting pulse rates of about 70 beats per minute. Superbly conditioned athletes have big strong hearts and resting pulse rates between 30 and 40. The maximum heart rate your body can endure for more than a short time is about 200 beats per minute. For the purposes of improving your cardiovascular system you need to get your heart rate between 130 and 180—and hold it there for at least 30 minutes.

You're probably overtraining or about to get sick if you wake up in the morning and your resting pulse registers four to eight beats above normal. Time to watch an old movie on TV and avoid the night life for a day or two.

Avoiding Winter Hazards

Despite what you may have read in the newspapers or in Jack London's old classics, very few winter travelers die from exposure to the elements or get buried in avalanches. They die because they fail to use common sense in emergencies. They fail to make the kinds of decisions that anticipate winter problems before those problems demand difficult solutions.

In this chapter, we'll talk about winter's most common safety hazards, debunk a few cold-weather myths, and discuss the rudiments of dealing with medical emergencies in the backcountry.

IT'S YOUR RESPONSIBILITY

The possibility of getting hurt five miles or five days down the trail shouldn't put a damper on fun; it just shifts the burden of responsibility for safety squarely on you and your companions' shoulders. After all, it's a long way to the doctor's office from the middle of the Boundary Waters Wilderness. You can't just pick up a phone and call in the ski patrol.

Self-reliance in the backcountry means that you become the doctor every time you ski away

147

Being lost in the woods is no fun. But with proper planning and a little common sense, you can avoid the scenario.

from touring center trail systems. Accept the idea as both a challenge and a responsibility. By acquiring a knowledge of proper first-aid techniques, you build confidence for handling problems in the backcountry. There's a world of truth to the old adage that "an ounce of prevention is worth a pound of cures."

Your education should start with a basic first-aid course such as those offered from time to time by the Red Cross or your local rescue squad or fire station. Be wary of classes geared toward home safety and the availability (within a short time) of medical assistance. Those courses of the "keep-the-victim-calm-and-wait-for-the-doctor" variety won't do you much good when you're dealing with a sliced finger in the middle of the Brooks Range. The farther off the beaten path you ski, the more you must rely on your own abilities to minimize winter dangers.

Reading a detailed first-aid text will also help. The best in my opinion is James Wilkerson's *Medicine for Mountaineering* (Seattle: The Mountaineers, 1977). The definitive handbook of medical and emergency evacuation procedures, the book provides insight in layman's terms on the physical and psychological consequences of cold, high altitude, burns, and other injuries.

Attitude Plus Aptitude

A broken ski tip, dark clouds gathering on the ridge, thin ice on ponds—none are dangerous by themselves. It is only a skier's *reactions* to these objective dangers that make them a threat to his safety. Fear and panic can cause you to make stupid decisions your normal common sense would never allow. But extreme nervousness in a difficult situation may not be totally controllable. The best we can do is to stay prepared for emergencies as a hedge against panic, the ultimate crippler of rational decision making.

Overdetermination is another backcountry attitude problem. Red-hot, goal-oriented skiers may set all kinds of records for land speed, altitude gain, and light pack loads on wilderness tours, but they are also likely to push companions too far too fast. The overachiever may be so reckless in his tireless pursuit of being first and fastest that he is completely indifferent to the abilities and needs of fellow skiers.

ROUTE FINDING

Route finding is the ability to recognize passing land forms, visualize the tiny contour lines on maps as three-dimensional objects, and constantly choose the safest route by correctly predicting what lies ahead. There are so many cues to follow on a winter ski tour that it is a rare occurrence when you need to use a compass.

The winter sun is a reliable direction indicator. From November to March the sun rises in the southeast and sets in the southwest. It sits in the southern sky at midday. At night you can also pick out the North Star and line it up with a pair of ski poles jammed in the snow. You'll have a true north bearing to follow in the morning.

Using Map and Compass

Although you may not always need them, always carry a map and a compass on backcountry ski tours. They're the only way to stay on course when the weather is bad or your route takes you through unfamiliar terrain.

Study the map carefully before setting out to avoid taking the wrong trails. Always take notice of your immediate surroundings and how they match your memory of the map when you're skiing so you don't get confused. The needle on a compass always points to *magnetic north,* not *true north.* Magnetic north is about 1,400 miles from the North Pole, so the compass needle points slightly west of true north in the eastern U.S. and east of true north in the western states. In the central U.S. the amount of difference (measured in degrees), or *declination,* is very slight. Magnetic north and true north appear very close together.

Declination is marked on U.S. Geological Survey topographical maps in a little diagram in the bottom left corner. A vertical arrow topped by a star points to true north on the map. The other arrow points east or west of the vertical arrow in the direction of magnetic north (marked MN). The degree difference between the two readings is printed to the right of the MN arrow.

In good weather, *orient* the map by lining up map symbols with distant objects such as peaks, hills, lakes, or valleys. Use the compass to orient the map so you can follow it in bad weather. Align the compass with one of the north-south lines on the map. (Point the direction-of-travel arrow or north symbol on the compass to north on the map.) Make sure the map is flat so you get an accurate reading from the compass. Don't let yourself be bamboozled by wild readings from your belt buckle or other metallic objects. With the edge of the compass baseplate on a north-south line, rotate map and compass together until the north end of the needle points away from you and toward (magnetic) north.

Now the final step. Rotate the map so the magnetic north-facing needle is angled the same number of degrees—and in the same direction east or west

Orient the map by lining up visual landmarks with those depicted on the map (left). Your map faces true north when the compass needle and the magnetic north arrow on the declination diagram line up the same number of degrees, and in the same direction, as they do from true north on the diagram.

of true north—as indicated on the map's declination diagram. Line up distant landmarks with map symbols. Stride boldly forth!

A word for those skiers who don't have one of the fancy orienteering compasses with movable dials, direction-of-travel arrows, digital readout, etc. You can still orient the map by taking a reading based on magnetic north alone. Orient the map by rotating map and compass together to magnetic north along the axis of the MN line on the declination diagram. True north lies east or west of this line, depending on the amount of declination indicated on the map.

Map Reading

Do you know how to read contour lines to tell the difference between gentle and steep terrain? Can you tell which way the river flows? Can you recognize avalanche danger? Skillful map readers can visualize what those funny, wavy lines mean and how they combine to represent a landscape worth traveling to for great skiing, or worth avoiding because of geographical hazards. Here are some positive signs to watch for when studying a map for safe skiing:

- Widely spaced contour lines indicating gentle terrain.
- Lack of green shading indicating treeless meadows or open slopes.

- Stream beds that show up as U's on maps with the apex of the U facing upstream. Ridges form V's between stream courses. Look for gentle ridges and valleys to follow. I like to follow ridges because you can stay out of the brush that usually lines streams, avoid avalanches, and soak in the scenery.

Here are some map signs to be wary of:
- Tightly packed contour lines indicating cliffs, avalanche danger, and tough, steep skiing.
- Narrow valleys that tighten into gorges (and waterfalls) from which retreat may not be possible.
- Circular hot spring symbols in the middle of lakes.
- Big rivers. Got a collapsible kayak in your pack?
- Steep north-south ridges and passes that may be passable in the dry seasons but blocked by cornices in winter. *Plan alternate escape routes for all these terrain situations.*

Getting Lost

It's happened to me, and it could happen to you. A buddy and I were lost for a day in a swirling blizzard somewhere near Cloud Peak in Wyoming's Big Horn Mountains a few years ago. We gave up studying a waterlogged, tattered topo map after spending an hour trying to locate ourselves in that rugged mountain world and, instead, pitched a tent.

At dusk the scratching of snowflakes against the tent fly eased for a moment and we scrambled outside in time to catch glimpses of Orion's Belt in the eastern sky and Polaris to the north. It was enough to put us on the right track the following morning. But we learned a couple of lessons on that tour about getting lost. Namely, don't waste time thrashing about in the woods like frantic bloodhounds, never move in the dark or heavy snowfall, and keep cool, sit tight, and think things through once the decision is made that you don't really know where you are.

CIRCUMNAVIGATING AVALANCHES

As the ski-touring landscape steepens from gentle foothills to alpine peaks, the likelihood of being swept up in an avalanche increases measurably. My advice is to keep your distance. Learn some respect. The alternatives are too frightening.

Five friends of mine set out on a trans-Sierra tour from Shepherd Pass to Kings Canyon in April 1982. They never made it.

It was snowing lightly when this group of experienced mountaineers reached the headwall below Shepherd Pass just west of Independence, California, on their first afternoon of skiing. The weather report had promised a clear crossing, but they decided to hold up anyway to see if the clouds cleared. The group set up two tents (one behind a large rock) about a mile from the top of the pass. They figured they had played it conservatively by camping so far from historical avalanche runouts.

The storm intensified, so the group settled in for an afternoon of card playing. When the wind picked up they built snow walls around the tents to minimize the buffeting. They all gathered in the tent shielded by the rock to wait out the storm. Late in the day a slab avalanche passed right over the rock like a tidal wave and buried the camp. One of the group members recalled that the group didn't even hear the avalanche coming: "We were all just pitched forward. I stood up through a torn seam, pushed some snow away, and could see no trace of our other tent. The avalanche had buried our packs and skis. We had no idea it could travel that far."

The stranded party stayed calm, however. They built snow caves, waited out the rest of the storm, dug out their skis and battered gear two days later, and skied happily home. But they were lucky. The same winter storm was responsible for the monster avalanche that buried the parking lot and base lodge chair lift station at Alpine Meadows, resulting in the deaths of seven skiers.

This story points up two features that almost all avalanches have in common: (1) *They follow paths they have taken before,* such as gulleys, open bowls, and chutes, (2) *The danger of avalanches increases during or after storms* and any time the wind blows more than 15 miles per hour—even under clear skies!

This book is not the place to learn about snow physics. For that, enroll in an avalanche avoidance clinic. For a couple of days follow an expert around the mountains who will teach you to dig a snow pit at the top of questionable slopes to check the stability of snow layers, and who will tell you what you can learn from studying snow crystals under a magnifying glass. He'll show you how cautious even the experts can be when traveling the backcountry.

Avoidance Techniques

If you don't cherish the idea of being knocked flat and then buried by a 200-mile-per-hour wall of white with the force of a freight train and the consistency of wet cement, then stay away from slopes between 30 and 45 degrees in

Prior to an avalanche, stress builds up in the snowpack like a stretched rubber band (left). Notice the downward pull on the small pines. The weight of a passing skier may be all this slope needs to avalanche. A small avalanche has already occurred in this area (right). There's only one safe route across—behind the ridge, far from overhanging cornices.

steepness, especially after storms. Avalanches either start as loose snow slides —that is, they start at a point and fan out—or start with a fracture line and slide as a single unit like a stack of dishes falling off a shelf. Big slab avalanches —fifty to five hundred or more feet wide—are the most dangerous. The whole shebang gives way with a crunch, then slides in tumbling blocks that can splinter three-foot-diameter pine trees as if they were toothpicks.

Avalanche avoidance is a skill you should acquire right away. The first lesson you should learn is to:

Never ski alone.
Never cross through the *middle* or *bottom* of a steep open slope.
Avoid cornices. Ski on the *windward* sides of ridges.
Stay away from 30- to 45-degree slopes after storms, or when it's windy.

And if you absolutely must ski in such areas? Be sure then to carry lightweight snow shovels, probe ski poles, and avalanche transceivers (such as Pieps, Ramer Echo II, and Skadi). But even then, don't confuse the fancy electronic gear with life insurance. Statistics show that, with or without beepers and shovels, you'll probably die or be seriously injured if a slide hits you. Before you cross a potential slide path:

Take pole straps off wrists.

Secure clothing: fasten all buttons and zippers and put on a hat.

Loosen your pack's waist strap.

Cross one person at a time.

Stay in the densest timber you can find.

If the snow cracks or collapses in front of your skis, turn around and ski to a safer route.

Finally, if you've taken every precaution and you still get caught:

Try to ski to the edge of the slide.

Discard skis, poles, and pack so they don't weight you down.

Call out to your companions so they can follow you.

Try to stay on top of the slide by "swimming."

When the slide comes to a stop, clear a breathing space in front of your face.

What to do if a buddy is buried? Mark the point where you last saw him and search the area as quickly as possible for any protruding clothing and gear. When you find him, be prepared to treat him for suffocation, shock, and hypothermia.

Snow stabilizes and settles over the course of a few days after a storm if the temperature rises and falls on either side of the freezing point repeatedly. But constant cold temperatures after a storm keep the avalanche danger high until the next freeze-thaw cycle. If you like to ski powder during storms, stay to the trees. And save the high-mountain tours for the settled snow of springtime.

Ski on the windward side of ridges to avoid avalanche hazards on mountain tours.

Lake inlets and outlets carry thin ice through most of the winter. Steer clear.

These lucky skiers (right) found a summer hiking bridge: do anything to avoid boots-off fording.

CROSSING THIN ICE AND STREAMS

Every year I take a tour to a lake in Jackson Hole, Wyoming, that freezes solid in early December then loses three feet of water over the winter. The unstable ice near the inlet and outlet claims the lives of several moose and elk every year. It's a wonder no skiers have suffered such a fate.

Swimming in February, attired in knickers, wool shirt, and long skis, is not my idea of a good time. Stay to the edges of big lakes and ponds. Should you ever break through—God forbid!—remove skis and poles as quickly as possible and pray that companions have the sense to reach out to you with linked-together skis and poles without plunging in themselves. Once you're out, replace wet clothes immediately, as you are well on you way to becoming dangerously hypothermic.

The best strategy for crossing streams safely is to plan your arrival—at the sturdiest snow bridges you can find—early in the morning when the snow is hard. Take pole straps off your wrists and release your pack's waist strap so you can wiggle free of it in case of a misstep. In late spring or when faced with wide streams, your only recourse may be to ford in bare feet. It's not as bad as it sounds. Just have a towel and foam pad handy for the drying process afterward.

PREDICTING WINTER WEATHER

Our insular twentieth-century lifestyle keeps us from noticing the simple natural signs that predict winter weather. For skiers there is great value in learning to read changing cloud patterns and wind currents for the messages they provide meteorologically. When you're out in the wilds, you can't just flick on the tube and lie back with a cocktail while some former-appliance-salesman-turned-TV-news-weatherman predicts snowfall amounts with radar and computer-aided satellite photos.

Storms are heralded by changes in atmospheric pressure. A ski guide who lives in northern Vermont claims that Mt. Mansfield, 30 miles west of his home, appears closer and more distinct just before a storm. You may perspire more heavily when skiing on days when storms approach. Why? A rise in humidity on such days almost surely spells lower barometer readings and snow to come. The air may take on a colder, fresher feeling as it whips your face.

What about clouds? Those thin, wispy high clouds called "mares' tails" foretell wet weather within twenty-four hours when they are followed by thin, high clouds. The same high clouds may leave a halo around the moon at night. If the wind shifts to the southwest, it's time to button up the tent flaps.

What about those supercold days when you wake up in the morning, the mercury is practically shivering in the bottom of the tube, and you have to light a hibachi under your car's engine block to get it started? If there's no wind blowing you're probably sitting under a huge high pressure cell and can expect several more days of chilly dry weather. North and northwest winds also mean cold, clear weather. West winds bring warmer weather.

Skiing in bad weather is tolerable with today's improved fabric designs in clothing and tents. But wait for extended periods of good weather in planning long backcountry trips. Plan shorter trips when the weatherman forecasts a storm.

THE SUN

It seems strange to think of the sun as a winter hazard when we worship its every ray on cold days. But the intense ultraviolet rays of springtime reflected off the snow surface—and at high altitude where there is less atmosphere to filter it—can cause painful sunburn, lip blisters, rob you of energy, and on long sunny days, give you a mild case of sunstroke. Your only protection in spring, when the danger is worst, is to wear desert white clothing, wrap your head like a Saudi Arabian oil minister, and apply 15-strength sunblock to exposed skin surfaces.

Snowblindness, or sunburned eyes, is another problem. Prevent it by wearing sunglasses even on overcast but bright days. The yellow-brown lenses currently popular allow good vision in a wide range of light conditions. Should you ever experience that nasty sand-in-the-eyes itchy feeling from too much direct exposure to the rays, sequester yourself in a dark room immediately and apply wet compresses to the eyes to relieve the pain.

Impromptu head wraps and sunproof shades are musts on spring tours.

The sun is a friend in the cold clear weather of midwinter. Take advantage of the solar-absorbing powers of dark colors like black, brown, and blue by wearing dark clothing to stay warmer. On snow camping trips, dark socks, sleeping bags, and pads dry out faster in the sun.

THE COLD

Maintaining a comfortable, stable body temperature is crucial to winter safety. But sometimes it's just not possible, as when a member of your party falls into a stream or a late winter rain soaks you to the bone. Barring such unforeseen disasters as these, try to change out of wet clothes (even if they're just sweaty) as quickly as possible, since wet clothes lose their insulating value and conduct body heat away. Carry dry clothing and extra gloves.

Hypothermia and frostbite often strike quickly, but not without warning. Stay alert to the warning signs and act quickly to avoid becoming a victim.

Hypothermia

Hypothermia is the medical term describing the mental and physical symptoms accompanying the chilling of the body core. It is also known as exposure—exposure to cold winds and damp clothing that can strip heat from the body so fast that no amount of shivering or jumping up and down can replace it. Most cases of hypothermia occur in air temperatures between 30° and 50°F.

But cross-country skiing is a heat-producing, self-propelled sport that will keep you plenty warm—at least until you stop. Then the body pulls blood away from the head, hands, and feet to ensure that the vital organs in the upper body stay warm. When it happens, you may not even be aware that you are slipping into the initial stages of hypothermia. You may deny it: "Don't worry, I'll be fine in a couple of minutes." This is no time for martyrdom, for soon your ability to speak clearly and make rational decisions will be impaired. Learn to recognize the following symptoms in yourself or your companions. Move fast, because the sooner you initiate the countermeasures, the less risk the condition will reach the point of no return:

Uncontrollable shivering
Slurred speech
Clumsiness, drowsiness, or apathy
Blue lips and weak pulse

Take care to change out of wet clothes and bundle up with an extra sweater or vest at the end of a tour. This is the best time to ward off hypothermia. Also be careful not to overextend the first few times you ski each winter. Feed frequently on carbohydrates and other high-energy snacks to fend off fatigue.

If someone in your party starts to go under, quickly set up shelter, remove all wet clothing, and replace with dry clothes. Since the hypothermic victim is past the point of being able to generate any heat for himself, it is crucial that he get warm liquids into his system. Light up a stove and heat water for tea. Don't give the victim any booze! Contrary to St. Bernard rescue techniques, alcohol causes any remaining body heat to rush to the skin surface and pass from the body, thus aggravating the situation.

If the victim is still shaking, put someone in a sleeping bag with him—sans clothing, as skin against skin works best. Fill a couple of plastic water bottles with warm water and rub the armpits, groin, and neck areas where large blood vessels are close to the surface.

Frostbite

The freezing of skin tissue resulting from a lack of blood circulation to the extremities is a problem for active skiers only when temperatures are very low. Frostbite first appears as a dull gray spot on the skin with an accompanying numb sensation. Don't rub the affected area or, worse, massage it with snow.

The best prevention is to stay in touch with your body. When fingers and toes get cold, swing your arms in a vigorous windmilling fashion and wiggle your toes. Change into dry socks or mittens if you have them. Put your hands under your armpits to get the circulation going again. If feet are extremely cold,

Check toes for frostbite when they first start to feel numb. Warm them against a companion's stomach.

stop, light a stove to make warm drinks, and put bare feet against a companion's warm stomach to get the blood flowing again. Frostnipped ears and cheeks can be warmed by pressing them against the top of your shoulder (tilt your head sideways to do this) or holding a warm hand against the affected area. Don't wait too long to do this.

When it is extremely cold, avoid bare skin contact with metal items such as ski poles and cameras, and use care in handling cooking fuel on winter camping trips, as the fuel, when spilled on fingers, can cause rapid chilling through evaporation.

ALTITUDE SICKNESS

Anyone who skis the high mountains has at some time suffered from altitude sickness, the general term describing a variety of bodily responses to underacclimatization and overexertion at altitudes above 8,000 feet. The scariest is pulmonary edema, a severe breathing problem characterized by fluid in the lungs. The coughing, wheezing, and chest pain of PE is often followed by pneumonia; fluid build-up in the lungs aggravates the problem of limited oxygen at high altitude by impeding the transfer of air between the lungs and blood. The only remedy is to help the victim walk or ski, or to carry him to a lower elevation.

It's common to feel a little spacey or headachy in the first few days at high places. We may experience sleeping difficulty, elevated pulse rates, and shortness of breath. The cardiovascular system works overtime to deliver a lesser amount of oxygen to the body. Some skiers experience stomach cramps and nausea.

Lie low the first couple of days up high. Take short ski tours. Don't race until you've acclimatized for at least three days. Take aspirin and drink plenty of fluids when you feel the effects of a strenuous day. Avoid drinking too much alcohol; it has a greater effect at high altitude and tends to dehydrate the body, further aggravating the symptoms. The only way to beat the altitude is to let the body adjust to it slowly.

EVACUATING INJURED SKIERS

The whole point of this chapter has been to avoid having to haul someone out of the backcountry. But sometimes we foul up. Recently, I heard about a skier who dropped a roll of film down a short couloir at Dewey Point in Yosemite. The skier scrambled down to pick up his film but couldn't climb back up. In desperation, one of his companions skied to the nearest road and called the National Park Service for help.

You can imagine the poor fellow's embarrassment when a helicopter arrived on the scene, deposited a crack crew of rescue climbers and medical aides, then lowered a litter down 20 feet of granite to save him. The cost of that rescue in fuel and man hours alone must have been enormous.

As a cross-country skier, you cannot depend on the airborne arrival of search and rescue teams; you must be self-sufficient. When a serious injury occurs, stop and make some sort of camp. Keep the victim as comfortable as possible. Get him inside a tent and wrap him in sleeping bags if you have them. Otherwise, supply the victim with any extra clothing you have. Plan your strategy. Are there enough skiers in the party to have two of them ski for help? Who will stay behind with the victim? Can you evacuate the victim yourself?

With common injuries such as sprained wrists or thumbs, keep pressure on the swollen area to keep blood from invading the tissue via ruptured blood vessels. I've seen skiers hobble out of the backcountry on sprained ankles. They wrapped the ankle firmly with an ace bandage and kept it loosely in the boot while two skiers, one on either side of the injured skier, supported the limping skier and the other party members carried packs and extra skis.

Shoulder dislocations are another common backcountry injury. Learn how to safely put the shoulder back into socket so the victim can ski out to the doctor. When shoulders pop out, the muscles that usually hold it in place will tense up and actually prevent the ball and socket joint from sliding back to normal positioning. The task is to overcome this muscle tension by applying gentle but steady outward pressure on the arm until the muscles fatigue, relax, and the shoulder pops back in.

When this happened to me on a long ski backpack trip several years ago, my skiing companion consulted a first-aid manual, placed his foot against my ribs in the armpit (on the same side as the affected shoulder) and gently pulled out on my arm. Luckily the bone slipped back into place without pinching any nerves or blood vessels, the biggest danger in reducing a dislocation by yourself. But if you're more than a day from civilization, who else is going to do it?

What about a broken leg? Set the leg straight and splint it with ski poles, branches and duct tape as best you can. Refer to the other leg to see what the broken leg should look like when set correctly. Make every effort to alleviate shock. If the accident happens only a short distance from the trailhead, the injured skier may be able to ski on one ski if supported by his friends. He can also be carried. Failing that, make a sled by lashing skis and poles together. Strap packs and pads on top, wrap the victim in a sleeping bag, and tie him on. With luck, you won't have too far to go, because improvised sleds slide poorly, fall apart, and are impossible to pull across traverses. You might be better off skiing out to secure the services of a toboggan, snowmobile or, yes . . . even a helicopter.

Forewarned is forearmed. If I haven't frightened you too much, you're now ready to deal with just about any disaster that could befall you and your companions on a winter tour. Don't worry. In all likelihood, the most threatening situation you will encounter on your ski tour will be getting caught somewhere without a corkscrew. Consider the nasty scenarios I've presented in this chapter as rare problems with simple solutions you will master with time and experience. Finally, the more you know about handling winter emergencies, the more likely you will be able to take the kinds of precautions that obviate drastic remedial measures.

FIRST-AID AND REPAIR KITS

You'd need a sherpa to carry a combination first-aid and repair kit large enough to handle every medical and mechanical problem you could conceivably encounter on a ski tour. Here's a list of a few items, though. You decide what you need to bring with you depending on the length of the tour, and the weather and terrain you'll be skiing in:

aspirin	extra food
Band-Aids	extra sunglasses
sterile gauze pads	waterproof matches
adhesive tape	knife
tweezers	compass
moleskin	space blanket
roller gauze	extra binding bail and screws
ace bandage	posidrive screwdriver
inflatable leg splint	clamp-on ski tips for wooden skis
prescription medicines	duct tape
sunscreen	epoxy and wire
first-aid manual	candle and flashlight

Pile snow into a mound to build snow caves in shallow snow (A). Pack it with skis or shovels (B). Carve a dome-shaped roof to support the snow load (C). A sleeping platform above the level of the entrance hole will stay considerably warmer than the outside air (D).

BUILDING AN EMERGENCY SNOW SHELTER

The Eskimos know it: Snow is a wonderful insulator. The air temperature inside a well-constructed snow cave or igloo never dips below the freezing point. Remember that fact if you ever get caught without a tent, get lost, or need shelter from a storm.

Ski tips don't make the best shovels for digging snow caves, but they'll do in a pinch. Look for snowdrifts on gentle slopes or dig into the side of a tree-well where the snow is at least six feet deep. Make a pile of snow if you have to and dig into it. Since digging a snow cave is wet work, attire yourself in appropriate waterproof clothing.

From a small entrance hole, dig slightly uphill and make a cavern-shaped room with a dome-shaped ceiling at least two feet thick to support the snow load. Make a platform for sitting and sleeping above the level of the entrance so cold air will seep down and out the door. Line the platform with packs and branches and huddle together with your pals for warmth. Try to catch a little shut-eye. Contrary to what Jack London says, you'll wake up shivering long before you're in danger of dropping off into the The Big Sleep.

A

B

C

D

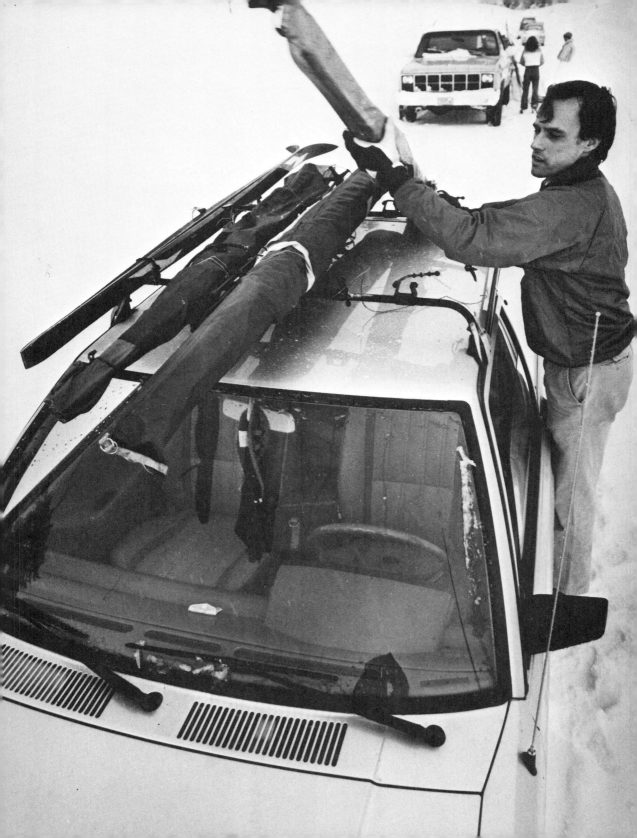

Winter Camping and Citizen Racing

Thousands of skiers will never hear the pulse-quickening drumming of skis on the starting line of a cross-country ski race. An even larger number will never spend the night outside in winter. They are missing two of the most rewarding experiences this sport has to offer.

After all, you can cover only so much ground on a day tour; at some point you must return to the trailhead. Have you ever wondered what kind of scenery awaited you around the next bend? With sleeping bag and tent in your pack, you have the freedom to explore our vanishing backcountry during its least populated time and lay claim to any part of it you want. No phones, no freeways, just you, the wind in the trees, and a million stars overhead.

Citizen racing also opens new horizons. It pushes you beyond physical limits you may not have believed yourself capable of. Planning to ski a race provides incentive for training and demands technical improvements in your skiing that make for savvy skiing in noncompetitive situations. The rush of adrenalin that even seasoned racers feel at the sound of the starting gun, the momentary apprehension before rushing downhill on super-thin racing skis at 25 miles an hour, are experiences not

165

Bag your skis on road trips to keep them clean.

to be missed. Snow camping and racing are not diametric opposites, just different experiences in the vast continuum of skiing. Both test your abilities to safely negotiate the winter environment, and each carries its own rewards

TRANSPORTING GEAR ON THE ROAD

Whether you and your friends are beating it down the highway to make the start of a citizen race, or racing across the country on a week-long ski trip, you'll be happier if you arrive there with ski gear intact. Get a good ski rack! Dropping three or four pairs of fiberglass skis into the path of approaching vehicles is a bit riskier than losing a load of Samsonite luggage under the same circumstances.

Zip your skis into a waterproof ski bag before tying them to the ski rack to protect the ski base from the grime and oil kicked up by passing traffic. Road spray will impede the bonding between ski wax and ski, and road salt will corrode metal ski edges. If you don't flush all the salt off the ski base with a liquid wax solvent at the end of the trip, it will melt snow to the bottom of your skis.

BEYOND THE DAY TOUR

Spring is the time for long ski mountaineering excursions and bushwacking adventures because you need plenty of daylight for leisurely picnics, daring downhill runs off remote peaks, or fearless forays into dense willow thickets where ski poles make handy machetes. The sun is low in the sky in midwinter, temperatures cold, and muscles still adjusting to a new season's activity. Keep day tours short the first few times you go out. Carry a small thermos filled with tea or hot chocolate. In planning tours, beginners should figure that they can

Camera fanny packs protect fragile photo gear on day tours.

travel approximately one mile per hour to allow plenty of time to reach their destination and return before dark.

Three types of day tours are possible: loop tours, up-and-back tours, or point-to-point trips (like river trips in summer, they are complicated by the need to hitchhike back to the starting point or shuttle cars back and forth). It's been my experience that you see different scenery on both loop *and* up-and-back tours (you just see it in reverse on the way back). Up-and-back tours also have the advantage that on your way out you can follow the neatly set tracks that you made on your way in. Obviously, none of this is a problem if you ski at a ski touring center that sets tracks and marks trails. If you prefer off-trail skiing, though, make a point of informing someone of your planned route, destination, and return time before each outing.

Skiers often ask how well they have to be able to ski before going on extended wilderness trips that call for a night or two of snow camping. A woman who was photographed in this book carried a thirty-pound pack and spent three nights on the John Muir Trail in the Sierra quite happily—and it was only her second time on skis. She had a solid, shuffling skiing style, was an experienced summer backpacker, and wanted to learn how to be comfortable sleeping outside in winter. A positive attitude toward the little inconveniences of camping on snow—namely, no swimming or sunbathing—is all you need to make the transition from day tours to longer treks.

TEN SNOW-CAMPING TIPS

The person who once made the comment that snow camping "is something a lot of people talk about, but few actually do" was right on the money. There are a couple of reasons for this. First, many of us place too much faith in equipment. We'd like to think the latest space-age fabrics, tents, and clothing will get us through the worst conditions. Only partially true. More likely, it's a combination of knowledge and experience rather than technological improvements in gear that will keep you comfortable on overnight tours.

Second, the tradition of wilderness "challenge" schools, whose approach to winter adventure is "cut a hole in the ice, dunk 'em and dry 'em," is the kind of guiding philosophy that's likely to make your first snow-camping experience your last.

1. *Slow down.* Take a gradual approach to the sport. The first time or two

If you find yourself continually skiing deeper into the backcountry, or far from the trail head at the end of a day tour, you're ready to try snow camping, a sublime experience if you approach the sport gradually the first few times you go.

you try sleeping outside in winter, set up your tent in the backyard or a half-mile from the car. One of my favorite snow-camping memories is a tent-bound night spent with a friend only a hundred yards from my home in Vermont. The northern lights came out after midnight and shimmered for two hours. They made a strange electric crackling sound I'd never heard before. It was mid-February, the temperature 25 below, and we needed three foam pads to keep the ice-cold tent floor from robbing too much body heat. I watched the celestial fireworks through a two-inch opening in the hood of my sleeping bag and was prepared to dash to the house in my bare feet if it got too cold.

If midwinter snow camping sounds too cold, plan trips for the spring to take advantage of long, high-mileage ski days and a spring sun so hot you can bake bread in a reflector oven. Of course, left unchecked, the rays can have the same effect on face, arms, and legs, but if you take the precautionary steps for dealing with the sun that I mentioned in the last chapter, you'll find it's great fun to loll around the stove in the morning waiting for the snow to corn up for afternoon Telemark contests, and by 2:00 P.M. still have plenty of time to make the next pass and put ten or fifteen miles under your boards before dinner.

2. So, having seen the good and bad of snow camping, I'll promise you're going to like it if you learn from the mistakes of the inexperienced. In short, avoid the mistakes, and keep warm, safe, and comfortable right from your first trip. That's tip number 2. Here are eight more tips to making winter camping more fun. They follow a natural progression in time, from selecting the right tents and packs, skiing to the campsite, setting up, to eating and breaking camp.

3. *Packs.* Use a soft or internal-frame pack for winter backpacking. Frame-type summer packs are too rigid for skiing and tend to throw you off balance, since the weight is carried too high on the back. In soft packs, load heavy items low and toward the back. Stow oft-used items and foam pads on top.

Soft packs hold loads close to the back to make skiing easier.

Fill water bottles every chance you get to ward off dehydration.

4. *Tents.* If you've visited a backpacking shop recently, you know that dome tents are the rage for winter camping because they are so roomy and stormproof. The wild variations on Buckminster Fuller's original geodesic-dome shape are so sophisticated that sun flaps and stove pipes are already passé. What's next? Nylon soft-water heaters, cable TV hook-ups, and conversation pits? What we really need are lower price tags on these babies!

Any tent with a waterproof nylon fly or Gore-Tex roof will work fine in winter. Some skiers prefer the light, peak-shaped tents that can be pitched with an avalanche probe ski pole. But more important: Can you pitch the tent in the dark when the wind is blowing? Can you pitch it with gloves or mitts on your hands? For winter, the less complicated and sturdy the tent, the better.

5. *Skiing to Camp.* "Prehydrate before you dehydrate." Drink like a camel every chance you get to prevent dehydration. Stop at every open stream and keep water bottles filled. What you don't drink during the day, you'll heat up when you first reach camp. In spring, carry a water bottle wrapped with black electrical tape to increase solar absorption. Tie the bottle to the outside of your pack. Keep filling your solar water bottle with snow to replenish fluids; the sun will melt snow into more water. In below-freezing temperatures, carry water next to your body to keep it from icing up.

Forget about high-performance waxing on snow-camping trips. Leave the race waxing kit at home. Instead, carry the simple two-wax systems (one canister for wet snow, one for dry). In spring, when snow conditions and temperatures are the most variable, augment your two-wax system by carrying a tube of red klister. (In midwinter, extra green and extra blue are the best bets, especially when applied in different thicknesses and kicker lengths.) Mountain skiers often wax the whole length of the skis for better grip. Better yet, they use climbing skins.

6. *Setting Up.* When you reach your destination, look for a campsite sheltered from the wind, but not directly under trees, as tents have yet to be developed that can deflect snow bombs and heavy branches. Avoid low valleys, meadows, frozen ponds, and any other areas into which cold air will sink at night. Don't park the tent in front of an avalanche path or expect to get much sleep if camped on top of a high, windy ridge—even though the view may be out of this world. Face the tent entrance downhill so cool night air won't rush in after sundown.

Change immediately into warm, dry clothes after setting up the tent. It's a good idea to put on everything you have: pile jacket, down vest, anorak, dry mitts, wool socks, down booties with nylon overboots, and warm hat. While one person arranges gear in the tent, someone should fire the stove to heat water for tea and hot chocolate and get a start on dinner. This is the most critical time of day in snow camping. Your body, low on energy reserves, cools quickly after vigorous skiing.

7. *Dinner.* You should eat at least 4,000 calories daily on a winter ski tour. Many winter campers find dehydrated foods too expensive and insufficient in terms of calories and nutrition for long winter trips. Whatever you choose to

Stamp down a level tent platform with your skis.

Nothing beats overboots worn over down booties to keep feet toasty around camp.

A dug kitchen (left) makes camp life comfortable. Food shelves, stove area, benches, steps, and imaginative cooking make this High Sierra kitchen (right) feel like home.

haul with you, take plenty of fats, oils, proteins that produce heat, and carbohydrates for quick energy. Vegetarians and health food folks beware: a basic snow-camping menu may not be for you. We're talking about cheese, nuts, sardines, peanut butter, crackers, salami, raisins, butter, jerky, etc., etc.

Keep dinners quick and simple with one-pot meals like macaroni and cheese. Another backcountry favorite is soup laced heavily with fresh vegetables, potatoes, noodles, garlic, and other spices. Experiment.

Use stoves that heat water fast. The Coleman Peak 1, Svea, and MSR stoves all work well. For four people, bring four quarts of fuel plus a tankful of gas for a week-long trip. Cut that figure in half for two people.

Always cook on some form of insulation, not directly on the snow. A small piece of ensolite foam works well.

Butane cigarette lighters make quick, waterproof stove lighters.

Remember to handle gasoline with gloves in extreme cold. Gas assumes the temperature of the surrounding air and will frostbite fingers if spilled on them.

Light stoves outside the tent to avoid igniting flammable tent fabric.

8. *Bedtime.* After that cold night in Vermont I always carry two foam pads to sleep on. Thin summer backpacking pads and air mattresses just don't measure up. You need, at the minimum, a full-length, half-inch-thick closed-cell foam pad to be comfortable.

Put boots in a stuff sack with a full water bottle and arrange them in the bottom of your sleeping bag so neither item freezes overnight. You can also dry socks and underwear by sleeping with them.

Which sleeping bags are best? Hooded, mummy-style sleeping bags with down or synthetic fills are a must. It is nearly impossible to keep any bag dry on long trips. So to maintain your bag's loft (and insulating ability) high, take it out of the stuff sack and dry it at every sunny opportunity—during breakfast, on lunch stops, and before bed.

9. *Food Caches.* Eating well on winter treks can often make the difference between having your trip be a movable feast or a desperate Donner Party dining experience. My friends and I have been leaving a well-stocked food cache in Yosemite's Tuolumne Meadows for years. Our hidden stash makes trans-Sierra crossings a breeze. Good food, no heavy packs to carry on multiweek trips.

We stock our food caches with a hearty supply of canned and bottled items that would be prohibitively heavy to carry: bourbon, pickles, canned enchiladas, pepperocinis, oysters, and beans. These culinary delights are then

Handle cold fuel bottles with gloves to avoid frostnipped fingers.

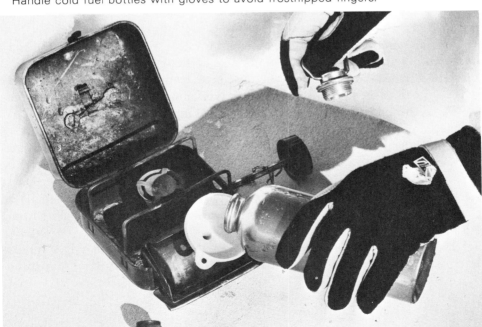

Dry sleeping bags on skis or trees at every sunny moment.

crammed into a heavy-duty plastic paint bucket, sealed with duct tape, and tied to the high branches of an inconspicuous tree. There's no worse fate than having a food cache stolen or munched by bears in early spring, but if you leave it somewhere for more than one season, better mark it somehow to indicate when you plan to claim it. One more warning: Avoid stashing gasoline in with the food, as it has the uncanny ability to creep into everything.

10. *Environmental Impact.* Soapy pot water tossed carelessly on the bank of a stream, human waste and toilet paper dropped on the edge of a frozen pond then covered with snow. . . . They don't seem to be problems when all is pristine white. But then the spring snow melt arrives and all the winter's carelessness comes rushing downriver to pollute our drinking water.

Organic matter doesn't decompose in a freezer. Inorganic items like Styrofoam and plastic containers may take thousands of years to break down. Always carry a sturdy trash bag on winter trips so you can pack food leftovers, cans, and paper. Find toilet sites as far from stream drainages as possible. Don't make fires with high-altitude trees, since the mountain ecosystem depends on the recycling of very limited organic materials; plants and animals cling to life with a fragile grip.

What about personal pollution? (And I don't mean chugging schnapps after a day of skiing.) Cooking stoves used inside tents throw off dangerous carbon monoxide fumes—as silent, sudden, and deadly a situation in tightly secured tents as leaving a car running in a closed garage. Keep your tent ventilated when cooking inside on blustery winter evenings.

WHY COMPETE IN A CITIZEN RACE?

Racing narrows the gap between how you ski and how you would like to ski. It's a sure-fire way to becoming a better cross-country skier. Of course, you can shuffle along forever and have a great time touring recreationally, but enter a citizen race and you suddenly find yourself in a situation where you must ski as gracefully and efficiently as possible, and hold a pace that allows you to maintain this technique for a long distance. Skiing quickly down hills and corners without losing time sharpens skills you'll use aside from racing.

Racing will give you the chance to practice everything you've gleaned from this book about equipment, technique, conditioning, and waxing. To be honest, your first race can be a glorious achievement—or a disaster. Even tested veteran skiers have unforgettable tales about their first races: backing over a shiny new pair of skis in the parking lot, burning a ski suit with a waxing torch, breaking a pole five kilometers into the race, missing a sharp turn and landing in an icy stream, falling down and being run over by a pack of cursing skiers. Sounds joyous, doesn't it? It usually is, at least in retrospect.

The races in our part of the country are some of the biggest social events of the year, probably because there is so much to laugh about when it's all over. The camaraderie and humor to be had competing with fellow skiers are worth ten times the entry fees paid to race organizers.

Types of Races

Like fun-runs on the road, citizen races are open to all skiers and most of the races are short—between 5 and 15 kilometers. They're a good choice, then, for first-time competitors. But the shorter races are bound to whet the appetite for longer-distance events and marathons (any race 50 kilometers or longer).

The 55-kilometer American Birkebeiner run from Telemark Lodge to Hayward, Wisconsin, every February is fast becoming one of the most popular citizen races in the world. Each year, about 8,000 skiers cross the starting line. The "Birkie" is the American entry in the ten-race international citizen marathon circuit (held in ten nations) called the World Loppet.

Of course there are longer races. The Minnesota Finlandia, a two-day 100-kilometer epic held near Bemidji, and the Canadian Ski Marathon, another two-day test in which finishers are awarded with the coveted *coureur du bois* ("runner of the woods") medal upon completing the distance from Montreal to Ottawa, are but two of hundreds of races held each winter in which the emphasis is more on finishing than winning.

Race Day Food

Eat lightly three or four hours before a race. Toast, oatmeal, and coffee, tea, or juice are sufficient. Lugging around a big ham and eggs breakfast in a short sprint-type race with plenty of anaerobic uphills could spell gastrointestinal disaster. Studies have shown that the body has plenty of fuel left over from the previous evening's meal and that heavy feeding before strenuous exercise diverts blood from the muscles to the stomach, which could cause cramping and nausea.

Arriving Early

The biggest mistake first-time racers make is arriving at the race site fifteen minutes before the gun sounds. Considering the number of details to be attended to before a race, you need almost two hours to accomplish everything in order that you arrive at the starting area relaxed—at least about the completeness of your preparation. Here's a checklist to follow on race day:

1. Arrive early and park near other racers so you can find out where registration takes place.

2. Pay your race fee and secure a bib. Pin it on right away.

3. Inquire at race headquarters if there are any indoor waxing rooms available.

4. Check your equipment to see that bindings are screwed in tight, poles sound (no cracks, baskets on tight).

5. Wax up. Waxing in the parking lot to the music of torches and scrapers is the cross-country equivalent of a football tailgate party.

6. Test-ski your wax on a slight uphill section of track. Do you have good grip? Good glide coming back down? Adjust kicker lengths. Scrape and change if you missed it.

7. Settle on a wax combination that works and stick with it, as it were, no matter that some wax sage says his triblend of hard waxes and klisters is just the thing. If you still want to make minor touch-ups on the way to the start, carry a small selection of waxes in a fanny pack that you can stow with your warm-ups right before the race.

8. Use the bathroom.

9. Stretch for fifteen minutes, then ski briskly for a couple hundred yards to get your heart used to pumping at a high rate and to warm up your muscles.

10. Find a place in the starting area equal to your abilities.

Warming Up and Cooling Down

Stretching before skiing to loosen the muscles you have built in training gives you the freedom of movement you need for fast, efficient skiing without the great risk of tearing muscles and tendons. Flexibility is as important a factor in good ski technique as balance and agility. The stretch poses on these pages are just a few of the many possibilities for relieving tension in the neck, back, legs, and upper body. Add a few warm-up moves of your own, and follow these guidelines for safe stretching:

- *Bring the muscle to tension but not to pain.* Start with slow movements. Don't bounce on the targeted muscle area; ease it gently through the full range of motion. You should feel a release in tension as the muscles gently let go.
- *The colder the day, the longer you should spend stretching.*
- *Stretching after skiing? You bet.* The last thing you should do is jump in the car after a race (or long tour for that matter) and cruise home. You'll pay for this mistake with sore muscles. Hard skiing builds up lactic acid levels in the muscles. Stretching and light skiing after a race will help the blood rid muscles of toxins such as lactic acid so you won't be hobbled in pain the day after a race. Be good to your body. Give it time to recover from the stress of a race to a semblance of physiological normality.

Racing is a sure-fire way to become a better cross-country skier.

Pre-Race Stretches

Neck muscle stretch.

Thigh stretch. Hold this pose for 30 seconds, then switch legs.

Back stretch. Twist slowly, gently.

Standing hurdler stretch to loosen thigh muscles.

Groin stretch.

Hamstring stretch. Hold this pose for 30 seconds. Don't bounce up and down.

Electricity fills the air as the gun goes off at the start of a citizen race.

The Start

Few moments in sport are as exciting as the start of a mass start citizen race. Nervous chatter fills the chill morning air. The wax. . . . The big hills and bobsled-run downhills ahead. . . . Suddenly the gun sounds and the mad charge of the blue-red-and-white brigade is under way. This is clearly no tea party. The moving mass of thrashing, bashing, elbowing, and double-poling skiers is not likely to disentangle for several kilometers. What to do?

Keep cool. Use the initial adrenalin rush to break away from the pack as much as possible. You need space to establish a pace. Keep your poles in close to your body so someone else doesn't fall on them and so faster skiers don't get clobbered on their way by.

Many first-time skiers burn themselves out too quickly in a race. If you haven't been training anaerobically but in a race find yourself charging up hills hot on the tails of better-conditioned skiers because of the excitement, you could "hit the wall" very early in the race. Resist the urge to let faster skiers dictate the pace. Find your own pace as quickly as possible and stick with it. Wouldn't you rather ski than do the dead-man shuffle across the finish line? The draining effects of a race are cumulative. Save your best shot for the last few kilometers where you'll need it most.

The best skiers can finish a 50-kilometer race in a little over two hours, but the average citizen racer takes between three and six hours to cover that distance. That's a long time to be moving the skis back and forth. Could you reasonably expect to finish a marathon even though you haven't been skiing very long? Are there ways to improve your chances? Yes on both accounts. Here's how.

Traditionally, the marathon season begins the third weekend in January and ends the third weekend in March. This schedule applies to the international citizens marathon league, the World Loppet, and its domestic counterpart, the Great American Ski Chase with its eight annual races in the U.S. If you want to race in a marathon this winter, begin a training program as soon as you can and do as much long-distance skiing through early winter as you have time for to build stamina for these long ski races. Here are a couple more recommendations to ensure success in your first race:

1. Follow the training advice outlined in the conditioning chapter in this book. Take long interval runs, lift some weights, ride roller skis, and pull on a rope exerciser right until the snow flies.

2. Ski every chance you get when there is snow. Intersperse short, fast, intense workouts to build your cardiovascular capacity with long-distance workouts to build the kind of endurance you'll need to ski continuously for four or five hours.

3. The race. There usually comes a time in marathons between 25 and 40 kilometers when your mind tells you, There's no way we can keep this up. These momentary depressions are hard to shrug off. My advice? Concentrate on skiing correctly even if you must slow the pace for a while. Stop at the next feed station and load up on goodies like cookies and orange slices. The only way to avoid low points in a race—and even veteran marathoners experience this feeling— is to prepare mentally and physically by chalking up lots of K's in training tours. Other strategies are calculated pre-race diets and frequent in-race feeding.

Pre-Race Diet

Although carbohydrate-loading was popularized by marathon runners in the 1970s, cross-country skiers were the first subjects of tests conducted by a Swedish physiologist who subsequently revolutionized the way long-distance athletes dine before races. The original studies revealed that if skiers "loaded up" on carbohydrates in pre-race meals, they could increase the amount of glycogen (stored carbohydrates) in the muscles that's used as fuel during an endurance race. This muscle fuel, glycogen, was found to convert to sugar (for energy) much faster than protein or fats. Good-bye steak and eggs, hello pasta, cereal, bread, corn, and potatoes: the new pre-race diet of marathon runners and skiers.

For races of 40 kilometers or longer, a modified carbohydrate-loading program seems to make sense. However, there is currently a trend away from overconsumption of carbohydrates to a more balanced pre-race diet that includes at least some fat and protein. A normal diet calls for food comprised of 50 percent carbohydrates, 35 percent fat, and 15 percent protein. (This is what the nutrition authorities say; most Americans overeat fats and proteins.) Proteins build muscles and cell walls. Carbohydrates are the source of quick energy. Fat ultimately supplies more energy than protein or carbohydrates but burns more slowly.

If you want to try a modified carbohydrate-loading program before a long ski race, try this "conservative" eating plan designed to boost performance but not be harmful to your system either by elevating blood sugar levels too high or damaging the kidneys through too frequent, too rapid glycogen depletion:

- The modified depletion phase of the carbo-loading program starts a week before the race with a *strenuous workout* in which you burn up all the glycogen your muscles have stored.
- For the next three days eat food with a higher percentage of fats and protein than normal, say 75 percent of your diet. Ease back on your training.
- Reverse this ratio in the last three days: Eat 75 percent carbohydrates, 25 percent proteins and fats. Treat yourself to a pasta dinner the night before the race, but watch the heavy meat and tomato sauce that may be hard to digest. Take a day or two off from training just before the race.
- Race day. Eat a light breakfast several hours before the race: tea, toast, a couple of flapjacks, and juice. The rest of your race-day feeding takes place on the trail.

In-Race Feeding

It's doubtful you could finish a marathon without feeding along the way. Feeding regularly at every feed station on the trail is the surest way to avoid

Stop every chance you get to chug food and fluids. The first two or three feed stations are critical to your success in long races.

hitting the wall with a resounding thud or succumbing to hypothermia. Hit every feed station, especially the first two or three. Don't mistake this as an invitation to an eating contest, just a recommendation that you banquet lightly but frequently on the orange slices, doughnuts, and fluid available. Eat, drink, and be on your way.

Feed stations are also a good place to touch up your wax. In marathons, many skiers carry a small fanny pack containing one or two waxes, a dry hat, dry gloves, a pint of light sugar-solution drink, and a few high-energy snacks such as nuts and raisins.

A word about caffeine. Some skiers swear by it; others get sick or *too* high when they use it. Olympic marathon champ Frank Shorter used to drink flat Coca-Cola on his runs. The U.S. cross-country ski team members often drink coffee before a race and many have experimented with time-release caffeine tablets. Studies have shown that caffeine switches the body from using glycogen as a primary energy source to "mobilizing" free fatty acids as fuel.

The process is this. Caffeine stimulates the body's production of epinephrine, which in turn triggers the metabolism of fat for energy. A little caffeine may provide just the lift you need when glycogen stores are low in the middle of a race. But watch out: it may lift you too high and send you crashing. Both in-race and pre-race feeding are areas of tremendous discussion among nutritionists, coaches, and athletes. Even the experts disagree as to what will work best to improve performance. Based on these suggestions, I'd suggest finding out what works for you. Always experiment with race-feeding programs on long training tours so you don't find that something disagrees with your system when you least expect or need it—in the middle of a race.

SKIING FOR JUNIORS AND SENIORS

As I mentioned at the beginning of this book: This sport is for everyone. For example, most of the marathon races we've discussed in this chapter incorporate shorter distances geared to the abilities of our younger and older skiers. The old German saying, "langlaufer leben langer" (cross-country skiers live longer), should also carry the message, "and they can start cross-country skiing as soon as they can walk."

The future vitality of this sport depends on how effectively we introduce it to the little ones. Children's ski schools such as those now in session at the Trapp Family Lodge in Stowe, Vermont, the Kinderski program at Telemark Lodge, Wisconsin, and Timberline Lodge, Oregon's SKIwee XC (a cross-country adaptation of *SKI* magazine's instructional program for young alpine skiers) are right on target. They stress the fun of skiing and follow a "games approach." Kids really go for "follow the leader," "hares and hounds," tag, and "kick the can" on skis. Young skiers don't need formal instruction. They learn best by mimicking adults.

Since this chapter plugs the benefits of competition, I should mention that kids thirteen and under can take advantage of the many Bill Koch Ski League programs that have been organized throughout the snowy north country. The Koch League stresses low-key competition (the program booklet's title says it all: "I hope I get a purple ribbon . . . because that's my favorite color.") and basic instruction in cross country and jumping. The Koch League has become a winter equivalent of Little League baseball in many communities. Inquire at your regional United States Ski Association office for the people to contact in your area.

Strongest testimony to the gentle, healthful qualities of cross-country ski-

Downplay the technical aspects of cross-country skiing with children; they'll take to it because it's fun. Get them acquainted with their skis indoors, then play games with them in the snow to introduce them to this lifetime sport.

ing is the number of skiers in their seventies and eighties still kicking down the trail. Montreal's Jackrabbit Johannsen is still skiing regularly at a hundred and seven. How many hockey, soccer, and basketball players continue playing into the golden years?

This is a lifetime sport, and one you can start at any age to enjoy its benefits. Anyone who walks or jogs in the winter will take to cross-country skiing. The USSA also has a program designed to introduce cross-country skiing to older Americans. It's called the Senior Pep League (Physical Exercise Pays) and by writing your local USSA office you can receive a free booklet that outlines specific conditioning and flexibility exercises, discusses basic clothing and gear selection, and touches on a few ski maneuvers.

This sport is fun, it's good for you, and—if you don't watch out—terribly addictive. Once you're hooked you may never want to stop. I plan to ski for the rest of my life. How about you?